DoDAF Wizdom

Planning, Managing and Executing Projects to Build Enterprise Architectures using the Department of Defense Architecture Framework

By

Dennis E. Wisnosky

with

Joseph Vogel

And The Other Wizards

Foreword by Dan Appleton

Copyright 2004-2005 by Wizdom Press
Printed in the USA.
All rights reserved.
No part of this document may be reproduced or transmitted in any form or by any means, electronic, mechanical, photocopying, recording, or otherwise, without prior written permission of Wizdom Press or Wizdom Systems, Inc.

ISBN# 1-893990-09-5

Third Printing.

Wizdom Systems, Inc.
1300 Iroquois Avenue Naperville, Illinois 60563
630-357-3000   Fax: 630-357-3059
Website: www.wizdom.com

DEDICATION

To the wonderful Military and Civilian People of the United States Department of Defense

They know very well that:

*We cannot solve our problems
using the same thinking that caused them.*
                                         - ALBERT EINSTEIN

Table of Contents

		Page
About the Authors		xi
Foreword		xiii
Introduction		xvi
Chapter One	Why the DoDAF?	18
Chapter Two	What Does the Customer Want?	32
Chapter Three	Minimalist Methodology	44
Chapter Four	IDEF Primer	60
Chapter Five	UML Primer	71
Chapter Six	Heading, Altitude and Airspeed *(Time, Cost and Quality based KPIs)*	85
Chapter Seven	DoDAF Products Unmasked	103
Chapter Eight	Let's Build an Enterprise Architecture	163
Summary and References		206
Appendix A	DoDAF Tools	216
Appendix B	Process Models to Data Models to Data Bases to Application Code	219
Appendix C	Glossary of Terms	229
Index		259

Table of Figures

Figure 1.1 The Transformation Plan is Key 23
Figure 1.2 OMB A-130 EA Elements 24
Figure 1.3 OMB Business Driven Approach 25
Figure 1.4 Component Base Architectures 28
Figure 1.5 OMB BRM 29
Figure 2.1 JCIDS 33
Figure 2.2 JCIDS Analysis 35
Figure 2.3 Essence of JCIDS Analysis 36
Figure 2.4 The new gates to navigate 37
Figure 2.5 Oversight Body Comparison 42
Figure 2.6 Joint interoperability directives and instructions 43
Figure 3.1: Three DoDAF Teams 45
Figure 3.2: DoDAF Product Organization 48
Figure 3.3: DoDAF Products by View 50
Figure 3.4 DoDAF Products by Tools Skeleton 55
Figure 3.5 DoDAF Minimalist Methodology Roadmap . 57
Figure 3.6 JCIDS Net Ready – KPP Documents Matrix . 58
Figure 4.1 IDEF Levels and DoDAF Views 61
Figure 4.2 Example of A-0 Level 62
Figure 4.3 Four ICOM Arrows in IDEF0 Model 63
Figure 4.4 Summary of "ICOM" Acronym Meaning 64
Figure 4.5 Example of Decomposition Hierarchy 65
Figure 4.6 Example of 3-Level Mechanism 66
Figure 4.7 Example of IDEF1X Model 68
Figure 4.8 Example of a Relationship 68
Figure 4.9 Types of Relationship Identifiers 69
Figure 5.1 Typical UML diagrams and packages 73
Figure 5.2 Use Case Symbology 74

Figure 5.3 Example Use Case Diagram 75
Figure 5.4 UML Activity Diagram Symbology 76
Figure 5.5 Example UML Activity Diagram 76
Figure 5.6 UML Class Diagram Symbology....................77
Figure 5.7 UML Class Diagram Example........................78
Figure 5.8 UML State Diagram Symbology 79
Figure 5.9 UML State Diagram Example 79
Figure 5.10 UML Sequence Diagram Symbology...........80
Figure 5.11 UML Sequence Diagram Example...............80
Figure 5.12 UML Collaboration Diagram Symbology 81
Figure 5.13 UML Collaboration Diagram Example 82
Figure 5.14 UML Component Diagram Symbology........82
Figure 5.15 UML Component Diagram Example............82
Figure 5.16 UML Deployment Diagram Symbology.......83
Figure 5.17 UML Deployment Diagram Symbology.......83
Figure 5.18 UML Deployment and Component Diagram Combined 84
Figure 6.1 N-KPP plan..89
Figure 6.2 OV-5 Operational Activity Modeling Methods..95
Figure 6.3 IDEF0 Indented List 96
Figure 6.4 KPI Analysis by Activity................................97
Figure 6.5 Time Analysis with MS Project.....................98
Figure 6.6 Sample Indicators table...................................99
Figure 6.7 Cross Product showing true labor by activity.100
Figure 6.8 OV-5 Swim Lane Diagram with example KPI 101
Figure 7.1 DoDAF Products and CADM........................104
Figure 7.2 AV-1 Template 106
Figure 7.3 AV-1 for our common example.....................107

Figure 7.4 AV-2 for our common example......................109
Figure 7.5 OV-1 Example..111
Figure 7.6 OV-2 Operational Node Connectivity............112
Figure 7.7 OV-3 114
Figure 7.8 OV-4 116
Figure 7.9 OV-5 IDEF0 Operations Activity Model 118
Figure 7.10 OV-5 Use Case Operations Activity Model .119
Figure 7.11 OV-5 UML Operations Activity Model 120
Figure 7.12 OV-6A Operational Rules Model.................123
Figure 7.13 OV-6b Operational State Transition
Description..124
Figure 7.14 OV-6C Event Trace Description. 126
Figure 7.15 OV-7 Logical Data Model 128
Figure 7.16 SV-1 Systems Interface Description.............131
Figure 7.17 SV-2 Systems Communications
Description..133
Figure 7.18 SV-3 Systems to Systems Matrix 135
Figure 7.19 SV-4 Systems Functionality Description......136
Figure 7.20 SV-5 Operational Activity to Systems
Function Traceability Matrix 139
Figure 7.21 SV-6 Systems Data Exchange Matrix 141
Figure 7.22 SV-7 Systems Performance Parameters
Matrix..143
Figure 7.23 SV-8 Systems Evolution Description 145
Figure 7.24 SV-8 for our common example 146
Figure 7.25 SV-9 Systems Technology Forecast 148
Figure 7.26 Systems Rules Model (SV-10a)....................150
Figure 7.27 Systems State Diagram (SV-10b).................153
Figure 7.28 Systems Event Trace Description SV-10c....155
Figure 7.29 Physical Schema SV-11................................156

Figure 7.30 Technical Standards Profile TV-1 159
Figure 7.31 TV-2 Technical Standards Forecast
Example 161
Figure 8.1 MANDROIDS on Patrol 164
Figure 8.2 Wizdom Minimalist Methodology Timeline..166
Figure 8.3 DoDAF Tools Recommendations 167
Figure 8.4 AV-1 170
Figure 8.5 Partial AV-2..171
Figure 8.6 MANDROID OV-1 173
Figure 8.7 MANDROID OV-5 Creation Process 176
Figure 8.8 MANDROID OV-5 A-0 177
Figure 8.9 MANDROID OV-5 A0 178
Figure 8.10 OV-5 Use Case 180
Figure 8.11 Use Case for the A0....................................180
Figure 8.12 MANDROID Process Flow........................182
Figure 8.13 Organizational Relationships Chart..............184
Figure 8.15 Systems Functionality Description 186
Figure 8.16 Physical Schema 187
Figure 8.17 Operational Event-Trace Description...........189
Figure 8.18 Systems Event-Trace Description................190
Figure 8.19 Operational Information Exchange Matrix...191
Figure 8.20 Operational Rules Model.............................192
Figure 8.21 Operational State Transition Description 194
Figure 8.22 System State Transition Description 195
Figure 8.23 Operations Node Connectivity Diagram.......197
Figure 8.24 Systems Interface Description
(Components)..199
Figure 8.25 Operational Activity to Systems Function
Matrix..200
Figure 8.26 Systems Data Exchange Matrix...................201

Figure 8.27 Systems Interface Description (Deployment) 203
Figure 8.28 TV-1 Partial Technical Standards Profile 205
Figure S.1 Enterprise Transformation 206
Figure S.2 Iceberg 207
Figure B.1: Context Diagram 220
Figure B.2: First Level Subprocesses from the Context Diagram 221
Figure B.3: WizdomWorks! Tools 222
Figure B.4: Logical Data Model Excerpt 223
Figure B.5: SQL Code Export 225
Figure B.6: SQL Code Generation 226
Figure B.7: Editing the Attribute Type 227
Figure B.8: Generating an ODBC Database 228

ABOUT THE AUTHORS

Some have said that **Dennis E. Wisnosky** managed the development of the first ever Enterprise Architecture and simultaneous creation of the first tools and methodology for building them.

Dennis founded and managed the USAF Integrated Computer Aided Manufacturing (ICAM) Program in the late 1970's. ICAM created the IDEFs (Integrated DEFinition language) and used both IDEF0 and IDEF1X to build an architecture of manufacturing for the entire Aerospace Industry.

Subsequently, Dennis went on to a career in the private sector and started Wizdom Systems, Inc. in 1986. He has amassed many honors and awards for his work both as an executive and as an entrepreneur.

Wisnosky has written 7 other books on BPR and Factory Controls. He has taught DoDAF and BPR around the world and continues to lead architecture projects. He holds degrees in Education, Engineering, and Management Science. He is a multiengine instrument rated private pilot and a PADI SCUBA Rescue Diver.

Dennis and wife Rosemary live in Naperville, Illinois and have 3 daughters and 6 grandchildren.

ABOUT THE AUTHORS

Few doubt that **Joseph M. Vogel (Joe)** has learned at the feet of a master. Joe has invested the last six years of his life mastering business process modeling and using automated modeling tools. While employed as a Business Analyst at Wizdom Systems, Inc. in Naperville, Illinois, and Washington, D.C., he has worked on many and varied projects.

Joe received his B.S. in Computer Technology in 1996 from Purdue University. Since graduation he has consulted with a number of private corporations and federal governmental organizations providing services ranging from web-based training development to process modeling to technical support.

Joe and his cat live in Elgin, Illinois. This is Joe's first venture into publishing. It will likely not be his last.

FOREWORD

It is often said by mathematicians that the primary value of mathematics is that it makes the invisible, visible. It is a language – albeit an arcane language to most mortals – which enables us to see and understand invisible realities like gravity, relativity, economics, chemistry, genetics and even the weather. Without the language, we would not only be blind to many of the realities around us that affect our very existence, we would be unable to have any affect on them, and consequently on our future – our survival.

Architecture is rapidly becoming to organizational thinking what mathematics is to the engineering of physical systems. It is a language whose purpose is to make the invisible, visible. With this language, we can articulate aspects of our organizational world like processes, information, knowledge, missions, capabilities, infrastructure, performance, and communications that have heretofore been invisible to the majority of us. Further, once we have learned this language, we can use it to <u>take charge of change</u> – as opposed to being its pawns.

But, there is more. Languages are the essence of thought. Without them, our ability to think about things in multiple dimensions, and therefore our ability to understand, communicate and collaborate, would be non-existent. Specialized languages increase in importance as we become more entangled in very complex environments,

FOREWORD

Thus, the language of architecture is a specialized language – attuned to enable us to cope with the increasing multi-dimensional complexity of the DOD and its environment – and to exact behaviors that manifest our visions.

This book is an important primer for the language of DOD architecting, the DOD Architecture Framework (DODAF). It meets three critical tests. First, it presents the language in context (rules and regulations of the DOD) and in specifics (the details of DODAF products). Second, by providing a minimalist methodology, it shows us how to use the language to think about the complex issues facing the DOD. Third, it digs into the mysteries of models – an important aspect of the architecting language – explaining both the role of models and the importance of creating "good" models.

But, this is not just any book. This is a book written by Dennis Wisnosky. Dennis is a true pioneer in the field of architecting – in fact, he is considered by some to be the father of structured organizational thinking in the DOD. Dennis began forging the trail to architecting in the early 1980s when his vision of the future was finally funded by the Air Force Logistics Command as the ICAM (Integrated Computer Aided Manufacturing) program. ICAM's purpose was to adopt structured thinking – the IDEF's

FOREWORD

(ICAM Definition Languages) were born here – to help understand not only how to engineer and build the Department's weapon systems, but to "improve the processes." ICAM was the cognitive model behind the TECHMODs – <u>Tech</u>nology <u>Mo</u>dernization programs used by the DOD to encourage Defense manufacturers to adopt CAD CAM and CAT technologies and tune their engineering and manufacturing processes to emerging concepts like concurrent engineering and manufacturing resource planning (MRP). Much of the logic and methodology behind what has become BPR (business process reengineering) in the DOD can trace its roots to Dennis's ICAM program. One thing is for sure: Dennis really understands. And, in this book, he shares his understanding with us.

Dan Appleton

INTRODUCTION

> "The Department of Defense will be managed in an efficient, business-like manner in which accurate, reliable, and timely financial information, affirmed by clean audit opinions, is available on a routine basis to support informed decision-making at all levels throughout the Department."
> Donald Rumsfeld
> January 31, 2002.

Welcome to <u>DoDAF Wizdom</u>, a book based on the United States Department of Defense Architecture Framework - DoDAF. This book will help you maximize the benefits that you and your organization can derive from building a DoDAF compliant Enterprise Architecture. The information in this book is based on knowledge accumulated over decades in performing Business Process Engineering (BPR) projects around the world in government and industry.

The DoDAF represents the accumulation of the work of many minds and many years. Its 2 volumes and desk book can be daunting. The DoDAF volumes act as a reference describing the intent of DoD. <u>DoDAF Wizdom</u> is written for those men and women who work on DoDAF Teams with a specific purpose.

<u>DoDAF Wizdom</u> describes the specific requirements for DoDAF products under the variety of circumstances that the DoDAF architect is likely to meet. It also introduces an 11-step methodology that demonstrates exactly how a DoDAF project should progress doing the amount of work that is no less and no more than necessary to get the job done.

To prepare for the building of these products <u>DoDAF Wizdom</u> includes primers on both the IDEFs and UML.

INTRODUCTION

Because of the requirement within the DoD to be more "business-like," <u>DoDAF Wizdom</u> also includes a chapter that the authors believe was left out of the DoDAF but is essential for the Joint Capabilities Integration and Development System (JCIDS) analysis to which Enterprise Architectures must comply at least at some level.

This is crucial because **Management Initiative Decision (MID) 913** says, "**Over time, metrics will become the analytical underpinning to ascertain whether the appropriate allocation of resources exists.**"

Finally, or perhaps essentially, <u>DoDAF Wizdom</u> provides an actual working example that takes the reader through application of what we call the Minimalist Methodology using a made up DoD example. In this example each product is produced in the logical order necessary to minimize rework by maximizing reuse of data as it is created. Some products are displayed as the result of computer based tools, but this is not essential.

We hope you enjoy this "guide book" and remind you that it represents a collaborative effort by the team at Wizdom Systems, Inc. As the reader of <u>DoDAF Wizdom</u>, you are the most recent addition to the Wizdom Family. We hope that you will be pleased with the book. Please visit our website <u>www.wizdom.com</u>, or email <u>dwiz@wizdom.com</u>.

Wizdom recognizes that the DoDAF and the laws, directives, regulations and guidance upon which it is built are evolving. Therefore it is Wizdom's intention to provide periodic addenda to registered readers of <u>DoDAF Wizdom</u>.

Chapter One

Why the DoDAF

When the eagles are silent, the parrots begin to jabber.
- Sir Winston Churchill

Why the DoD Architecture Framework?

Why an Enterprise Architecture (EA)?

It is practically a full time job keeping up with the various organizations working on Enterprise Architectures and the tools and methods to support them. A partial list includes:

> OMG MDA
> IEEE 1471
> TOGAF
> ISO RM-ODP
> OASIS BCM
> ICH Value Chain
> S.A.I.L.
> BMPI
> GAO FEA

Some might argue that the goal of these EAs is to implement Information Technology (IT). IEEE 1471 says this specifically. However, IEEE 1471 also goes on to very

---

Enterprise Architectures resulted from recognition that a top down plan is necessary for bottom-up implementation to succeed.

elaborately describe "Stakeholder Viewpoints" and admit, "Now this is what it is all about" in section 4.2.1.4 of the reference cited for Chapter one at the end of this book.

Because the efforts of these Organizations are a moving target, it is suggested that the reader go to the Summary and References chapter URLs for additional most recent information. This book focuses discussion on the Federal Enterprise Architecture (FEA) as being most relevant to the DoDAF. Then, it moves on to the DoDAF.

"DoDAF Version 1.0 is an evolution of the Command, Control, Communications, Computers, Intelligence, Surveillance, and Reconnaissance (C4ISR) Architecture Framework, Version 2.0, dated 18 December 1997, and supersedes it" (John Stenbit memo of 9 February 2004)

C4ISR was brought about by command, control and communications issues discovered in the first Gulf War. In many ways C4ISR became the design tool set for the concept of Network Centric Warfare (NCW) which is to ride on the evolving Global Information Grid (GIG).

As DoD moved to turn the GIG concept into reality, the Internet was rapidly transforming management of industry and government and providing revolutionary approaches for how industry and government could be managed and operated. The Clinger-Cohen Act (CCA) of 1996 took a page out of the books on Business Process Reengineering (BPR).

"The FEA is a business and performance-based framework to support cross-agency collaboration, transformation, and government-wide improvement. It provides OMB and the Federal agencies with a new way of describing, analyzing, and improving the Federal Government and its ability to serve the citizen."

What is BPR?

Business Process Engineering (BPR) seeks to transform an organization from its problematic AS-IS state to its TO-BE state with lower cost and higher performance.

BPR requires top managers to determine their true organizational goals, examine how the organization truly functions, or does not function, and then engineer a direct course for building processes to realize those goals. BPR can be accomplished by answering four simple questions.

What is the ideal process model for your business goals?

Four Simple Questions	Phase of Work
What business are we in? What business do we want to be in? What expectations do we have for improvement?	Strategic Goal Assessment
What do we do to accomplish our goal?	Process Modeling and Analysis
What do we need to know, to do what we do?	Data and Information Modeling
When do we need to know, what we need to know, to do what we do?	Workflow Modeling and Analysis

Clinger-Cohen demands proof of Business Process Reengineer-ing.

The Clinger-Cohen Act of 1996 (CCA) seeks this same information for all functions of the Federal Government.

What is the Clinger-Cohen Act?

CCA asks what came to be known as "the three pesky questions":

"Is the function the asset will support tied directly to our agency mission?

Could another agency, government or private entity do the job better?

Have our processes been reengineered to give the best performance at the lowest cost?"

> The CCA of 1996 instituted the process of requiring that Government be run in a business like manner.

Although CCA was passed in 1996, as is typical, it took several years for the Act to be understood and to be translated into actionable regulations in each Government Organization. The Office of Management and Budget (OMB) is responsible for administering CCA.

<u>Office of Management and Budget Circular No.A-11, Exhibit 300, Part I, Section I.C. Performance Goals and Measures</u> require a submission of information about each investment that will be expending $1M or more in that budget year. This report is intended for the OMB to meet its statutory responsibilities under a number of Acts.

> With publication of A-11, it could be argued that OMB for the first time began to live up to its Management responsibility as well as its budgets responsibility.

Together, CCA and the Government Performance Results Act of 1993 (GPRA) intend to identify and quantify every process of Government. This is the same goal as BPR in the private sector, that is, the business sector. In fact, today it is common to talk about the business of Government, or the business that a Government unit performs.

Related to GPRA and CCA are: Federal Acquisition Reform Act (FARA) of 1996. Paperwork Reduction Act (PRA) of 1995. Federal Acquisition Streamlining Act (FASA) of 1994 Government Management Reform Act (GMRA) of 1994. CFO Act of 1990. And, various Circulars Particularly OMB A-130.

The Federal Government Chief Information Officer (CIO) Council set out in 2000, under the auspices of the Administrations E-Gov Initiative, to set the stage for an Enterprise Architecture for the entire Government - the Federal Enterprise Architecture (FEA). OMB took up the challenge as the structure that would make E-Gov (Services to the Citizen and Agency Interoperability by Internet) possible and for the rationalization of every function of Government.

According to the OMB: *"The FEA is a business and performance-based framework to support cross-agency collaboration, transformation, and government-wide improvement. It provides OMB and the Federal agencies with a new way of describing, analyzing, and improving the Federal Government and its ability to serve the citizen."*

What is an Architecture?

- Merriam-Webster online has 5 architecture definitions. The one that suits our purpose most closely is: "The manner in which the components of a computer or computer system are organized and integrated." Replace the word computer with the word business and it becomes: *The manner in which the components of a business or business system are organized and integrated.*

- The USAF Integrated Computer Aided Manufacturing Program (ICAM) had an all-inclusive definition of architecture: "A commonly accepted model of an organization, an industry or an enterprise. The model is based on and built by an integrated set of tools and methods which support creation, deployment, operation and disposal of the model and the system which is its embodiment."

- DoDAF says: "the fundamental and unifying structure defined in terms of elements, information, interfaces, processes, constraints, and behaviors."

- OMB Circular A-130 says: "An EA is the explicit description and documentation of the current and desired relationships among business and management processes and information technology."

These architecture definitions imply the need for many parameters to completely describe the architecture, including: risk, decisions, data, systems, components, organizations, functions, requirements, performance, and more.

All of these architectures show us how to work with models representing the past, the present and the future.
Each is supported by tools, methods, and processes.

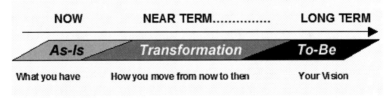

Figure 1.1 The Transformation Plan is Key

Architecture is the bridge from the AS-IS to the TO-BE.

Architectures support life cycle models and the methods to build and maintain them.

An entire book could be written on the Transformation Paradygm and at least a chapter on TO-BE Architectures. Here the reader is left with just the notion.

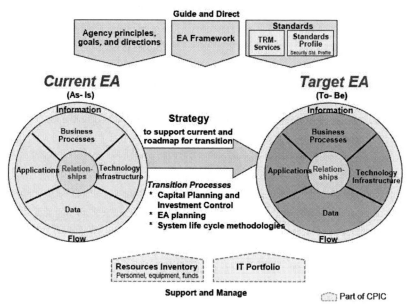

Figure 1.2 OMB A-130 EA Elements.

This OMB picture of EA Elements is a powerful statement. It contains the notion of Framework, Strategy and Transition. These are supported by Reference Models. As shall be seen, OMB A-130 can be mapped to the DoDAF.

First, let's review some fundamentals.

What are Reference Models?
Reference Models must match their purpose. In Judaism and Christianity, a reference model for all human beings may be Adam and Eve. Reference Models can serve as a framework for integration, a point of departure, a good

Reference Models are starting points for discussion about a particular TO-BE situation – there is no one size fits all.

beginning, something to copy exactly or more. Reference models contain specifications for how objects within the model link together or communicate. Think of building an object out of LEGO^R while looking at a picture. The end result could be exact, an extension, bigger, smaller. Several people could each have the same picture and agree to build parts of the same model. Because the reference model defined standards, the objects would fit together.

OMB defines Five Reference Models. Each is for a different purpose. Like the LEGO^R example above, they are intended to work together to support the OMB "Business Driven Approach."

The OMB is taking a top down business driven approach to the FEA.

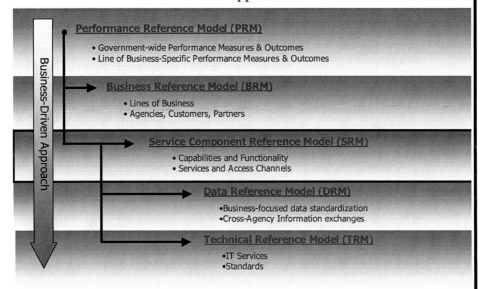

Figure 1.3 OMB Business Driven Approach

Because this is a book about DoDAF and not about the FEA, the details about these definitions are skipped. Instead, please go to the OMBPMO website and other references for the latest information.

Why is the OMB FEA important to the DoD and the DoDAF?

The FEA provides guidance for playing by the rules. Without complying there will be no money for future work – period.

How to comply with the FEA?

First:
- For FY 2005, A-11 requires agencies to align to PRM v1.0, SRM v1.0, TRM v1.0, and BRM v2.0.
- Major IT investments must align to the BRM, PRM, SRM, and TRM. Non-major IT investments must align to the BRM.
- Beginning in FY 2005, agencies should use the PRM for new development, modernization, and enhancement of major IT investments.

While there can be some exceptions, CCA gives OMB the authority and the power to deny funding.

Is it compliance for compliance sake?

No it is not – the FEA provides technical value.

- Whether it is business or government or the business of government, the network centric world is here. Organizations are truly virtual. Recently an international technical publication postulated the world in the near term in which every person and every object has its own Internet Address.
- The globalization of business is supported by global standards. Think the LEGO^R example where there are precise definitions for how the blocks interface.
- The tools and methods are beginning to exist so that engineers can focus on building their objects and the network does the rest. The DoDAF calls this "one to net." The FEA refers to component-based models within component-based architectures.

What is a Component Based Architecture (CBA)?

Officially a CBA is: "An architecture process that enables the design of enterprise solutions using pre- manufactured components. The focus of the architecture may be a specific project or the entire enterprise. This architecture provides a plan of what needs to be built and an overview of what has been built already."

The key term here is pre-manufactured component. The idea of a CBA is that **it is** what describes the detailed process work. Each component is a business process – the job of war fighter or the job of the payroll clerk. The CBA interacts with the SRM – the Service Component Reference model to integrate those Components necessary

Components are like the LEGO Blocks.

Prebuilt software is assembled to perform applications necessary to fulfill the business objectives.

The Component builder believes that: If we build them, they will buy them

Reference models can be studied, copied, replicated, built upon and even ignored. Then can be simple or complex. There are no right or wrong reference models. The only rule is, "do they suit their purpose."

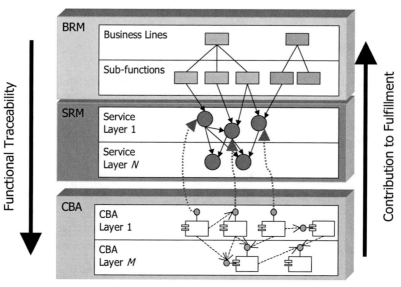

Figure 1.4 Component Base Architectures

to perform the business of the enterprise as described in the BRM – the Business Reference Model. In the BRM, the focus is on the business, not on technology.

In the OMB FEA, the BRM reports to the PRM – the Performance Reference Model – that describes the value of the business process. The Data Reference Model (DRM), and the Technical Reference Model (TRM) serve supporting roles.

How will it really work?

The Project team, after it understands the AS-IS problems and TO-BE requirements goes to a catalog of components and picks pre-manufactured solutions. How these solutions work together is predetermined by their design according to technical standards. What they do, why they do it, and when they do it is based on the purpose for the business functions existence and will be detailed in the transition or transformation plan.

As was said, C4ISR and DoDAF drafts preceded the OMB/FEA and the Federal Enterprise Architecture Framework (FEAF) drafted by the CIO Council working on E-Gov. Treasury and other agencies also build their own Enterprise Architectures.

But, by definition, OMB/FEA as the keeper to the keys to the vault, is now the mother of them all. That is, all FEAs must show how they fit into the OMB FEA. There is a DoD placeholder within the OMB FEA BRM.

DoD architectures must intersect with the OMB FEA BRM

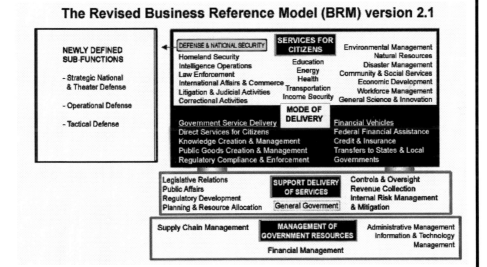

Figure 1.5 OMB BRM

Where is the DoD Placeholder?

The placeholder for DoD is in the function called "Defense and National Security."

This is primarily where the business of DoD will be integrated with the other business of Government. However, it must be understood that there will be other points of interaction – Social Security with DoD payroll, for example.

Returning to the question asked at the beginning of this chapter: **Why the DoD Architecture Framework?** – it is now known that there can be several answers.

Business architectures were born of necessity as interactions within and between organizations became too complex to be managed without a plan and a roadmap to execute the plan.

Frameworks provide tools and methods that allow architectures to be built from various viewpoints or perspectives in a way that predetermines interoperability.

OMB, faced with the Congressional Mandate to enforce CCA which says in part: "coordinate, integrate, and, to the extent practicable, establish uniform federal information resources management policies and practices in order to improve the productivity, efficiency, and effectiveness of

---

DoDAF is the practical State of the Art of 2 decades of architecture, tools and methods work in both the public and private sectors.

federal government programs and the delivery of services to the public," responded with the FEAF and the FEA.

DoD, faced with the need to build C4ISR, developed a framework of tools and methods where each of the various constituent teams could solve their own problems in ways that would work with the results of others.

As it became clear that the business of DoD is more than C4ISR, a broader approach was mandated to morph the C4ISR Framework into a holistic DoD Architecture Framework for all of the business of DoD.

To achieve the OMB goal - One window into the workings of Government for the external citizen customer and the internal Government customer – there must be a DoDAF.

To achieve the DoD goal that is now described as "born joint" there must be a DoDAF.

> OMB FEA and DoDAF have the goal that all processes and all systems are "born joint" - e.g. with the ability to communicate as appropriate.

Source: Deputy Chief Information Office (DCIO)

Chapter Two

What Does the Customer Want?

Give the lady what she wants.
- MARSHALL FIELD
I not only use all the brains I have, but all I can borrow.
- WOODROW WILSON

> The customer must comply with the DoDAF, link to the FEA and comply with Clinger-Cohen.

What does the customer want? Marshall Field and many others have struggled over this question. Within the DoDAF environment the answer is often – "I will know it when I see it." Of course, this is after the money has been spent and is therefore usually not an acceptable answer.

DoDAF Wizdom takes the position that what the customer wants is to get the money and the authority to get what he or she wants. Having a wonderfully crafted Enterprise Architecture is not the purpose of a project – getting the funding to improve a process or build a system is the purpose.

The facts are that the OMB gets to rule on Clinger-Cohen compliance and that for an integrated architecture between 7 and 26 DoDAF products are needed. The DoDAF is only the means to the end, not the end.

Fortunately the DoD 5000 Acquisition Policy Revision and the Joint Capabilities Integration Development System (JCIDS) provide the guidance needed to help the customer decide what is needed to get the money. The revised DoD 5000 policy objectives are:

- **Streamline the Process**
- **Increase Flexibility**
- **Enhance Business Practice**
- **Emphasize Evolutionary Acquisition**
- **Integrate Acquisition Business Model with a transformed Requirements Generation System**

The revised 5000 series together with the DoDI 6210.01D describes the DoD goal that all systems be "born joint."

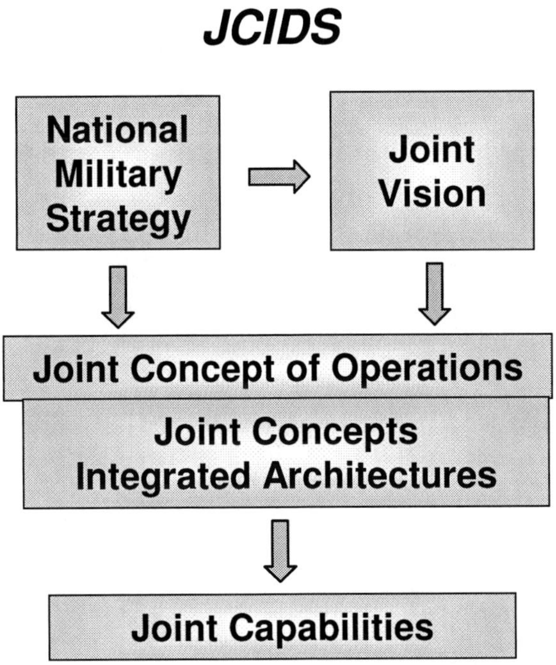

JCIDS

```
National Military Strategy  ⇒  Joint Vision
          ↓                        ↓
     Joint Concept of Operations
     Joint Concepts
     Integrated Architectures
                ↓
        Joint Capabilities
```

Figure 2.1 JCIDS

The rules of DoDAF engagement are in flux – vigilance is advised.

In the words of the DoD, "JCIDS replaces the Bottom up, often Stove Piped Requirements Generation System (RGS)." JCIDS procedures are established in the JCIDS support the Chairman of the Joint Chiefs of Staff (CJCS) Instruction CJCSI 3170.01D.

CJCSI 3170.01D with some exceptions and caveats: 1) Eliminates the Capstone Requirements Documents (CRD), 2) Eliminates Mission Need Statements (MNS), 3) Dispenses of Operational Requirements Documents (ORD).

> CJCSI 3170.01D, DoD5000 Policy and CJCSI 6212.01D are key to getting the customer what he or she wants.

JCIDS intent is to implement a "capabilities driven approach" to the acquisition process. As such, DoD specifies an "evolutionary" "spiral development process" for all systems. On the one hand JCIDS links tightly to the new requirements of the war fighter and on the other hand "priorities established through the JCIDS process should provide a basis for the science and technology community to focus developmental efforts as specified in the Joint Warfighting Science and Technology Plan (JWSTP)."

CJCSI 3170.01D makes it clear that integrated architectures are key to the "born joint" paradigm and especially key to successfully navigating the process of selling a program and keeping it sold.

> Dust off your CIM models and get out your BPR books.

Born Joint begins with top down Strategic Policy Guidance. In time, this Guidance will include Joint Operating Concepts, Joint Functional Concepts and Integrated Architectures. Because both the new acquisition model and

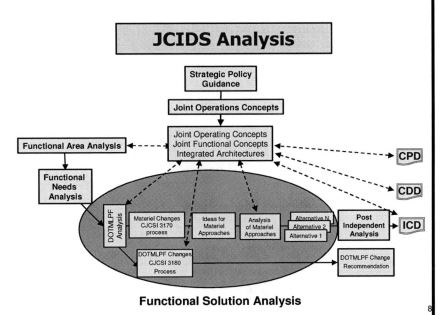

Familiar Procedure, but new documents required.

Figure 2.2 JCIDS Analysis

JCIDS recognizes that these architectures do not yet exist, and that there are many evolving and interim procedures.

The revised procurement policies and the JCIDS are all about managing the outcomes. JCIDS asks, what should be the outcome in a given situation?

As JCIDS sees it, finding out what the customer wants, or more realistically fitting what the customer wants into the DoD EA, begins with Functional Area Analysis (FAA). The reader connecting with the Yogi's "déjà vu all over

We can use the familiar IV Phase BPR approach for the JCIDS Analysis.

Phase II is for understanding the business – AS it IS. Phase II tries out very changes through analytical techniques and locks in on the TO BE business processes and systems if necessary. The vee shape is to symbolize that there is a profound difference in the AS IS and TO BE thought process.

again," is well on the way to understanding what the customer wants.

Today, DoD calls this a "capabilities oriented approach." Those who have done BPR in the private sector or worked on the many DoD Corporate Information Management projects, or their offspring, will see immediately those concepts of the JCIDS of "Top – Down analysis, Functional Area Analysis, Functional Needs Analysis (FNA) and the Bottom-Up Functional Solutions Analysis (FSA) are well

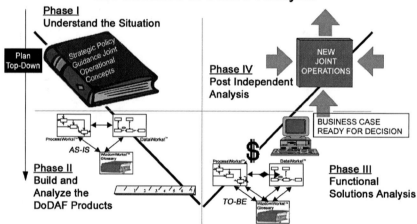

Figure 2.3 Essence of JCIDS Analysis

grounded by this previous work. JCIDS goes from here to a very structured procurement process and provides an oversight wrapper called the Functional Capabilities Board (FCB) that completes the Post Independent Analysis (PIA). What is new is the need to produce specific products during the AS-IS and TO-BE analysis, and preparation for working with the FCB during the PIA. Further, JCIDS places new emphasis on both being compliant with the full range of Doctrine, Organization, Training, Materiel, Leadership and Education, Personnel, and Facilities (DOTMLPF) solutions in order to advance joint warfighting and providing a means of recommending changes.

Getting the customer what is wanted is as simple as producing the new documents at the right time and in the right format. These documents can be mapped to the DoDAF as will be shown.

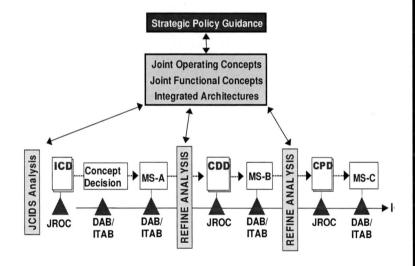

At least three documents are necessary for the procurement process.

Figure 2.4 The new gates to navigate

What are the Documents and when do I need them?

From this picture it appears that the documents follow JCIDS Analysis – this is a trap. As will be seen in Chapter 3, the documents are directly mapped to DoDAF products. They are produced according to the well-known procurement milestones, but their content is discovered during JCIDS Analysis.

What are the Documents?

- Initial Capabilities Document (ICD)
    - **Necessary for Milestone A**
    - **Replaces MNS**
    - Identifies a capability gap or other deficiency
    - Describes evaluation of DOTMLPF approaches
    - Support Analysis of Alternatives (AoA), Concept Refinement and Milestone A
    - Not updated once approved

- Capability Development Document (CDD)
    - **Replaces ORD at Milestone B**
    - Identifies operational performance attributes of proposed system
    - System specific, applies to single increment (in an evolutionary program)
    - Results from Technology Development and supports Milestone B

- Updated or rewritten for subsequent increments

- Capability Production Document (CPD)
    - **Replaces ORD at Milestone C and FRPDR**
    - Identifies production attributes for a single increment of a program
    - Prepared during System Development and Demonstration
    - Rewritten for each increment in an evolutionary program

- Capstone Requirements Document (CRD)
    - **No Near Term Change**
    - Describes overarching thresholds/goals and standards in functional areas
    - Useful for family-of-systems or system-of-systems approaches
    - Developed only at JROC direction
    - Eventually will be replaced by integrated architectures

The JCIDS is a work in progress. Pay attention to its instant status.

Who is the Customer?

The ultimate customer is the US Tax Payer followed by OMB. However, during the time of a specific DoDAF project there will be many, many DoD customers. The instant customer is of course whoever is paying the bill for the project. If the customer doesn't know what he or she wants, it is suggested to follow the advice Dennis always gave to his

Be sure that you understand customer needs vs. customer wants.

children – "figure it out." It all worked out very well for them.

Who is the Customer's Customer?

This is a good time to get out your LOA – List of Acronyms. The answer is in the previous figure – it depends on the evolutionary development process.

JROC is Joint Requirements Oversight Council.
DAB is Defense Acquisition Board.
ITAB is Information Technology Advisory Board.
Those familiar with the former acquisition process will see that Concept Refinement and Technology Development become separate phases prior to Milestone A.

Perhaps this chapter should be titled, "What does the Customer Need." The customer may think that he or she wants an Integrated Architecture or DoDAF products, but what the customer needs is for his or her program to make it through these milestones.

What is a Joint Potential Designator?

Every DoDAF product, especially the 5000 series documents should be considered proposals. JCIDS provides for 3 proposal designators depending on its degree of "jointness." They are:

- JROC Interest – could be any proposal that the JROC decides to review.
- Joint Integration – applies to those proposals that require intelligence, munitions or interoperability certifications.
- Independent – those proposals that have no direct impact on the joint warfighter.

Joint designation determines who validates and/or approves a proposal. The decision as to what designator makes the most sense and when is based on many factors. On a point scale of 1 to 10, 8 are the politics of the situation. Pay attention.

Who is really in charge of all of this?

The answer again is, it all depends. There is new function known as the JCIDS Gatekeeper. The function of the JCIDS Gatekeeper is to ensure that proposals are evaluated for joint warfighting impact and assigned to the correct staff for analysis and coordination. See the comments above.

Power of the Gatekeeper includes determining the joint potential designator, the lead Functional Capabilities Board (FCB), and the lead Joint Warfighting Capability Assessment Team. Note that the joint potential designator can be reevaluated as each document is produced.

> Think of St. Peter when thinking of the JCIDS Gatekeeper.

> Committees, committees and more committees.

Oversight Body Comparison

Joint Requirements Panel (JRP) 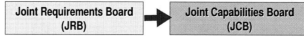 **Functional Capabilities Board (FCB)**

- Services
- DIA Representative (Intelligence Supportability)

- Services
- Combatant Commanders
- USD (AT&L)
- USD (I)
- USecAF (Space)
- ASD NII/ DOD CIO
- D, PA&E
- DIA Representative (Intelligence Supportability)
- Mission requirements board Executive Secretary
- Advisory Membership
  - J-6E/I (Interoperability Advisor)
  - J-8 Warfighting Concepts and Architectures Integration
  - DOD Laboratories & Industry

Joint Requirements Board (JRB) → **Joint Capabilities Board (JCB)**

Figure 2.5 Oversight Body Comparison

The FCB replaces the Joint Requirements Panel from the old 5000 series. The FCB has considerably expanded responsibilities and membership. The Joint Requirements Oversight Council remains. The Joint Requirements Board (JRB) becomes the Joint Capabilities Board (JCB).

Responsibilities of the FCB include that new capabilities be developed with a joint warfighting context; that proposals are consistent with the joint force as described in the joint operating concepts and validating Joint Impact proposals. The first FCB was to support the Joint Forces Command. Others have been formed and are being formed. Knowing that the FCBs will exist, other Governance Boards are being stood up with the goal of ensuring DoDAF compliance leading to born joint capability.

OK, I get it – What does the customer really want?

The ultimate answer is to survive the Government FEA process. Within DoD, the answer is to appear as a line item in the Program Operating Memorandum – the POM.

Getting the customer what he or she wants could take years.

The next chapter describes what a "Minimalist Methodology to do this.

Is JCIDS the end of the story for Born Joint?
Nope! Joint interoperability directives and instructions from DoDI 4630.8 show that there are many masters of this process. And they are constantly changing. The reader is advised to reference this guidance and always ask – "What does the customer want"?

We know that we belabored the customer wants thing. **What if the customer does not know what he wants?** Remember the real purpose for the EA – to figure out the right thing to do.

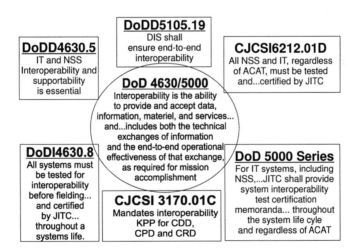

Figure 2.6 Joint interoperability directives and instructions

Chapter Three

Minimalist Methodology

In challenging times when ethics are more important than ever before, make sure you set a good example for everyone you work and live with.
-Ralph Waldo Emerson

This chapter will focus on doing no more and no less than truly required to build an architecture based upon the DoDAF. The DoDAF document Version 1 like the C4ISR frameworks which proceeded, seems to take pride in the fact that there is no prescribed methodology. The assumption is that either the Government or the private sector has its own and can adapt. Given, that DoDAF can be viewed as 21st Century BPR in Uniform, this is true to a certain extent. However, experience has proven that starting a BPR project without a methodology is like beginning a cross-country trip without a road map – only worse. Therefore, DoDAF Wizdom leaves the reader with a methodology wrapped around the DoDAF products necessary for what the DoDAF calls an "integrated architecture," plus those necessary for compliance with the JCIDS. And, because many of the DoDAF products can be based on UML, additional products that are practically gimmees, as they say in golf. They are also included.

Further, it is suggested to the reader that Chapter 3 and Appendix A of <u>BPR Wizdom – A Practical Guide to</u>

Managing BPR Projects is extremely relevant to this chapter. That information is not repeated here except to say:

1) Have a strong project name
2) Have three interconnected teams

DoDAF projects should have three levels of interaction and team play.

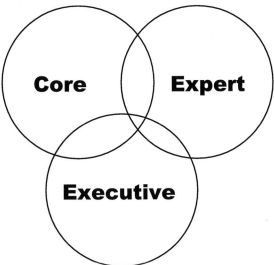

Figure 3.1: Three DoDAF Teams

3) Have total buy in on your methodology
4) Have a schedule that is detailed to your methodology with many check points and deliverables
5) Automate data collection and product building and management to the maximum extent possible.

Teams of 7 to 13 members work best.

Each of these 5 points has been learned the hard way by the authors and many others.

Lessons learned from Claude Shannon's Information Theory and the book <u>The Mythical Man Month</u>, tell us to limit the size of the team. Extremely large projects are conducted by multiple teams of 7 to 13 people with clear rules as to how their results are to be integrated. Pick a name that is a call to action. Pick a combination of tools.

> Reading BPR Wizdom Chapter 3 is strongly encouraged.

Appendix A of the first edition of <u>BPR Wizdom</u> had 35 Tools Vendors. Two years later, the second edition also had 35 Tools Vendors, but half had changed. Appendix A of DoDAF Wizdom also has Tools Vendors and a discussion of each. Choose wisely and heed the advice that multiple tools will be required from multiple vendors.

Now, on to the minimalist methodology. How to present this is somewhat of a conundrum because one could begin with a discussion of DoDAF products, which would be confusing because they are based on some combination of IDEF, UML matrices and tables that must also be understood. Or, one could begin with IDEF and UML with no context for why this is important. Or one could set the context based on DoD guidance and fill in the blanks later. This later approach is that of <u>DoDAF Wizdom</u>. This chapter:

    1)   Displays the complete list of DoDAF Products

2) Distills this list to the products essential for an "integrated architecture"
3) Adds products required for compliance with NCOW and 6212.01D as of this writing
4) Outlines a DoDAF project roadmap in a makes sense sequence of product builds.

What is a View?

Views are sometimes called perspectives. Views are based upon the concept that person sees the world based upon a particular purpose at a particular time. As the saying goes, "to a person with a hammer, all the world looks like a nail." This is this person's view of the world - his or her hammer view.

DoDAF has 4 views. Each view can produce 2 or more products specific to the purpose of that view. The hammer view would include a variety of hammers.

In the DoDAF the views are Technical, Operations, Systems and All. There are a total of 26 products in the 4 views. The products and the views are each related quite specifically with one another within the views and rather loosely between the views.

The views are intended to depict the goals and interests that might be relevant to that view. The products describe

DoDAF includes 26 possible products organized in "Views." Each View can produce 2 or more products.

View depends upon the tools at hand and the intended purpose.

How many total products are there? 13+2+2+9 =26 products. The same as the number of letters in the English Alphabet.

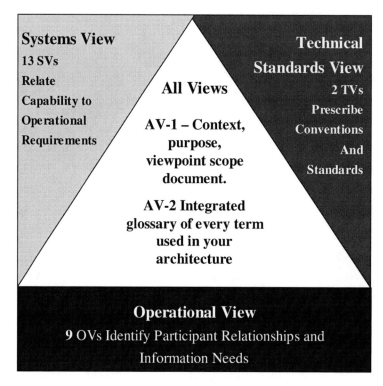

Figure 3.2: DoDAF Product Organization

Here are some of the relationships between the views: The Operations View contains products that describe the work that is done by the organization that is the subject of architecture.

- The OV transfers to the SV: What Needs to be done; who does it and the information exchange required to get it done.

- The OV transfers to the TV Operations Requirements and Capabilities.

The Systems View contains products that describe the hardware and software performing or helping to perform the operations.
- The SV transfers to the OV Systems that support the operations and information exchanges.
- The SV transfers to the TV Specific systems capabilities required to satisfy information exchanges.

The Technical View contains products that describe both AS-IS and TO-BE technology supporting operations and systems.
- The TV transfers to the SV Technical standards criteria governing interoperable implementation procurement of the selected system capabilities.
- The TV transfers to the OV basic technology supportability and new technical capabilities.

The All Views products contain the basic roadmap governing the EA, which is being built, and the glossary of every term used in the EA precisely as it is used. DoDAF refers to this as the EA taxonomy.

Let's look at the official DoDAF complete list of products.

> Views are interconnected by the specific information that is transformed between them.

Applicable View	Framework Product	Framework Product Name	General Description
All Views	AV-1	Overview and Summary Information	Scope, purpose, intended users, environment depicted, analytical findings
All Views	AV-2	Integrated Dictionary	Architecture data repository with definitions of all terms used in all products
Operational	OV-1	High-Level Operational Concept Graphic	High-level graphical/ textual description of operational concept.
Operational	OV-2	Operational Node Connectivity Description	Operational nodes, connectivity, and information exchange needlines between nodes
Operational	OV-3	Operational Information Exchange Matrix	Information exchanged between nodes and the relevant attributes of that exchange
Operational	OV-4	Organizational Relationships Chart	Organizational, role, or other relationships among organizations
Operational	OV-5	Operational Activity Model	Capabilities, operational activities, relationships among activities, inputs, and outputs; overlays can show cost, performing nodes, or other pertinent information
Operational	OV-6a	Operational Rules Model	One of three products used to describe operational activity- identifies business rules that constrain operation
Operational	OV-6b	Operational State Transition Description	One of three products used to describe operational activity- identifies business process responses to events
Operational	OV-6c	Operational Event-Trace Description	One of three products used to describe operational activity- traces actions in a scenario or sequence of events
Operational	OV-7	Logical Data Model	Documentation of the system data requirements and structural business process rules of the Operational View
Systems	SV-1	Systems Interface Description	Identification of systems nodes, systems, and system items and their interconnections, within and between nodes
Systems	SV-2	Systems Communications Description	Systems nodes, systems, and system items and their related communications lay-downs
Systems	SV-3	Systems-Systems Matrix	Relationships among systems in a given architecture: can be designed to show relationships of interest, e.g. system-type interfaces, planned vs. existing interfaces, etc.
Systems	SV-4	Systems Functionality Description	Functions performed by systems and the system data flows among system functions
Systems	SV-5	Operational Activity to Systems Function Traceability Matrix	Mapping of systems back to capabilities or of system functions back to operational activities
Systems	SV-6	Systems Data Exchange Matrix	Provides details of system data elements being exchanged between systems and the attributes of that exchange
Systems	SV-7	Systems Performance Parameters Matrix	Performance characteristics of Systems View elements for the appropriate time frame(s)
Systems	SV-8	Systems Evolution Description	Planned incremental steps toward migrating a suite of systems to a more efficient suite, or toward evolving a current system to a future implementation
Systems	SV-9	Systems Technology Forecast	Emerging technologies and software-hardware products that are expected to be available in a given set of time frames and that will affect future development of the architecture
Systems	SV-10a	Systems Rules Models	One of three products used to describe systems functionality - identifies constraints that are imposed on systems functionality due to some aspect of systems design or implementation
Systems	SV-10b	Systems State Transition Description	One of three products used to describe system functionality - identifies responses of a system to events
Systems	SV-10c	Systems Event-Trace Description	One of three products used to describe system functionality - identifies system-specific refinements of critical sequences of events described in the Operational View
Technical	TV-1	Technical Standards Profile	Listing of standards that apply to Systems View elements in a given architecture
Technical	TV-2	Technical Standards Forecast	Description of emerging standards and potential impact on current Systems View elements, within a set of time frames

Figure 3.3: DoDAF Products by View

This is the complete set of choices. DoDAF goes from here, very quickly to "7 essential products necessary for an integrated architecture." This is the beginning.
The 7 are:

AV-1 Overview and Summary Information
AV-2 Integrated Dictionary
OV-2 Operational Node Connectivity Description
OV-3 Operational Informational Exchange Matrix
OV-5 Operational Activity Model
SV-1 Systems Interface Description
TV-1 Technical Standards Profile

It is best to interpret these seven to be the minimum set of DoDAF products for any EA, not only for "integrated architectures." The differences will be the degree of completeness of the products.

But, this is the beginning, not the end of the minimalist methodology. Along came Network Centric Operations Warfare (NCOW) and CJSCI 6212.01 discussed previously and said: "Interoperability and integration of IA solutions within or supporting the DOD shall be achieved through adherence to an architecture that will enable evolution to network centric operations and warfare by remaining consistent with the DOD Architecture DoDAF, and defense-in-depth approach." This means more products.

Added to the list for NCOW are:
OV-1 High-Level Operational Concept Graphic

DoDAF says there are 7 "essential products for an integrated architecture."

However, for all practical purposes, a DoDAF compliant EA requires at least 15 products for Interoperability Certification.

Sidebar:

DoDAF Product new math.

26 complete.

7 for integrated.

The 7 + 5 for NCOW = 12.

The 12 -2 + 3 for CJSCI 6212.01 = 13.

But – see the previous side bar. Plan for 15 minimally.

DoDAF does not advocate a particular methodology to build the products.

SV-2   Systems Communications Description
SV-3   System-Systems Matrix
SV-4   Systems Functionality Description
SV-5   Operational Activity to Systems Function Traceability Matrix

CJSCI 6212.01 eliminates SV-2 and SV-3, but adds:

OV-4   Organizational Relationships Chart
OV-6c Operational Event Trance Description
SV-6   Systems Data Exchange Matrix

This leaves 15 products that are considered the minimum for an DoDAF NCOW CJSCI 6212.01 compliant architecture. **The question on the table is how to build it.**

DoDAF offers this : *"The DoDAF does not advocate the use of any one methodology (e.g., structured analysis vs. object orientation), or one notation over another (IDEF1X or ER notation) to complete this step (build the products), but products should contain the required information and relationships."* So, the team gets to decide its own methodology. What should it be?

The DoDAF offers guidance in that it points to both the IDEFs and to the UML as the notation for many DoDAF products. Additionally, the Core Architecture Data model is built on IDEF1X as defined by FIPS pub 184.

All of the above fits into one picture for a minimalist methodology. But this requires a little understanding of the

IDEFs and the UML. This is started here, but it is covered in more detail in later chapters.

What are the IDEFs?

IDEF (Integrated DEFinition language). IDEF began as the syntax and semantics necessary to build integrated architectures for manufacturing – that was 1976 during the USAF Integrated Computer Aided (ICAM) Program. The idea was to be able to integrate the best practices of all the aerospace manufacturers. To do this tools and methods, collectively known as the IDEFs were established to form teams, manage projects and to build various models of activities and data that could be combined for various purposes. IDEF remains the most widely used modeling and analysis technique in the world.

IDEF consists of IDEF0 for process modeling and IDEF1X for data and information modeling. IDEF0 is Federal Information Processing Standard (FIPS) Publication 183. IDEF1X is Federal Information Processing Standard (FIPS) Publication 184. IDEF0 has been used in hundreds of government projects to model processes, activities and functions. IDEF1X is used to build both information and Data models. The DoDAF CADM is an IDEF1X model.

What is the UML?

The UML was developed in the 1980's, no one knows quite when or by whom or even why. Its alleged purpose is for

IDEF and UML, the true essentials.

The IDEFs are covered by FIPS Publications. UML is managed by the OMG.

software design, development and deployment. The idea of UML is to use an "object orientation" whereby objects, the things, including us, which exist in the world inherently know how to interact to accomplish a particular purpose. Of course the catch here is that the world and the objects must first be modeled so that what they are and their allowable interactions are is fully understood. Whereas the IDEFs are complete with a methodology, like the DoDAF, the UML prides itself in being devoid of methodology. However, the UML goes even further. Even though, an organization known as the Object Management Group (OMG) professes to manage UML, inherent in the UML are concepts that allow the UML notation to be anything an individual thinks is a good idea.

UML has many variants and dialects. There are 9 basic UML model types. Some of these models are combined into 'Packages.' UML also has the concept of 'abstractions' and 'stereotypes' so that anything can be a UML model. <u>DoDAF Wizdom</u> bases its UML on Sam's <u>Learn UML in 24 Hours</u> – i.e. in 24 1-hour sessions.

The DoDAF volumes reference both the IDEFs and the UML as "templates" for various products. The DoDAF standardizes on products, but it doesn't standardize on a process for producing those descriptions (a well-defined order of activities, a set of artifacts produced and ways to monitor or control the work) – this is the missing methodology that is now introduced as minimalist.

Then, an example of an architecture built minimalistically is shown.

DoDAF Product	Product Name	Use Case	Activity	Class	Object	State Chart	Sequence	Collaboration	Deployment	Component	Matrix Form	IDEF0	IDEF1X	Simulation
AV-1 ☺	Overview and Summary Information											●		
AV-2 ☺	Integrated Dictionary											●		
OV-1 △	High-Level Operational Concept Graphic	●										●		
OV-2 ☺	Operational Node Connectivity Description							●						
OV-3 ☺	Operational Informational Exchange Matrix										●			
OV-4 △	Organizational Relationships Chart	●		●										
OV-5 ☺	Operational Activity Model	●	●									●		
OV-6a	Operational Rules Model												●	
OV-6b	Operational State Transition Description					●								●
OV-6c ☐	Operational Event Trance Description						●							
OV-7	Logical Data Model				●								●	
SV-1 ☺	Systems Interface Description								●	●				
SV-2	Systems Communications Description										●			
SV-3	System-Systems Matrix										●			
SV-4 △	Systems Functionality Description	●		●								●	●	
SV-5 △	Operational Activity to Systems Function Traceability Matrix													
SV-6 ☐	Systems Data Exchange Matrix										●			
SV-7	Systems Performance Parameters Matrix										●			
SV-8	Systems Evolution Description										●			
SV-9	Systems Technology Forecast										●			
SV-10a	Systems Rules Model												●	
SV-10b	Systems Site Transition Description					●								
SV-10c	Systems Event - Trace Description						●							
SV-11	Physical Schema				●								●	
TV-1 ☺	Technical Standards Profile										●			
TV-2	Technical Standards Forecast										●			

☺ The Essential 7 △ NCOW ☐ CJSCI 6212.04

Figure 3.4 DoDAF Products by Tools Skeleton

Triangles and squares indicate added NCOW and 6212.01 products. Smiley faces indicate DoDAF products essential for integrated architecture.

The essential 7 products are identified with a **smiley face** just to the right of the DoDAF product name in the Minimalist Methodology. NCOW products added are indicated by a triangle and 6212.01 products added are indicated by a square. At the top are either IDEF or UML model types that could be used to build these products.

How does the team know which products to build when?

The "which products" answer is easy. The team can build only the ones labeled as being essential for an integrated architecture or required for NCOW or 6212.01. However, as shall be seen, by following the logical plan, some additional products are created with little or no additional work – so why not build them?

The DoDAF volumes show several possible product build and dependency sequences. The authors' opinion is that much of this advice reflects the background and the politics of the various creators of the DoDAF. However, this DoDAF advice is the most practical:

- *"After the **Operational Activity Model (OV-5)** is developed"* <u>*"The products are each dependent on **OV-5** but not on each other.*</u>*"*
- *"Each labeled graphical item (e.g., icon, box, or connecting line) in the graphical representation of an architectural product should have a corresponding entry in the integrated dictionary."*

This gospel of the OV-5, the truths surrounding AV-2 above, the need for a document establishing the context purpose and viewpoint – the AV-1 and the need for a picture showing the current understanding and intent – the OV-1 should substantially provide the minimalist methodology direction – and it does.

STEP #	STEP NAME / WORK PRODUCTS / DURATION
1	Develop Overview and Summary Info AV-1 AV-2
2	Build Operational Activity Models OV-1 OV-5
3	Build Org. Relationships Chart, Logical / Physical Data Model, and Systems Functionality Descriptions OV-4 OV-7 SV-4 SV-11
4	Build Operational Event Trace Description and System Event Trace Description OV-6C SV-10C
5	Build Operational Informational Exchange Matrix OV-3 OV-6A
6	Build Operational State Transition Description and Systems State Transition Description OV-6B SV-10B
7	Build Operations Node Connectivity Diagram OV-2
8	Build Systems Interface Description (Components) SV-1
9	Build Function, Tractability and Data Exchange Matrices SV-5 SV-6
10	Build Systems Interface Description (Deployment) SV-1
11	Build and Maintain the Technical Standards Profile TV-1

Figure 3.5 DoDAF Minimalist Methodology Roadmap

The Minimalist Roadmap actually has more than 15 products. This is because, as our examples will show later, some products can be derived from others with little or no additional work.

Figure 3.5 is the Minimalist DoDAF Methodology Roadmap. Massive efficiency is gained by transferring information as it is logically developed from one product into the next product. Looking at the figure it can be seen that certain products are continuously developed during the project. The AVs for example have both AS-IS and TO-BE purposes as does

TV-1 and the Activity Models. After the IDEFs and UML products enable initial understanding, information is reused and cross-checked as the architecture evolves.

How do I know that my Minimalist Methodology produces a compliant architecture?

Continue to cross check against evolving DoD DoDAF Doctrine. This is the last thing done in this chapter through the CJCSI 6212.01 product documents matrix of figure 3.6.

Document	Net Ready Key Performance Parameter Products															NCOW RM	KIP Compliance	IA Compliance
	DoDAF Products																	
	AV-1	AV-2	OV-1	OV-2	OV-3	OV-4	OV-5	OV-6c	SV-1	SV-2	SV-3	SV-4	SV-5	SV-6	TV-1			
ICD		X														X		
CDD	X		X			X	X	X				X	X	X	X	X	X	X
CPD	X		X			X	X	X				X	X	X	X	X	X	X
CRD		X			1		2									2	2	2
ISP	3		3	3		3	3	3				3	3	3	3	3	3	3

X is required, 1 is old CRDs updates, 2 is new CRDS, 3 is ACAT, Non ACAT and Fielded Systems. Net-Ready KPP Products produced for the CDD will be used in the ISP.

Figure 3.6 JCIDS Net Ready – KPP Documents Matrix

This chapter reduced the 26 DoDAF products to 15 for an architecture that will be:

- Integrated with the 7 essential products
- Compliant with NCWO
- Compliant with JCIDS for joint.

Nevertheless, remember: What does the customer want? Answer should be to do the right thing right. What is that thing?

Analysis of the Architecture should tell the team. And, as these products are built and analyzed, the right thing could change and or the right way could change.

Which brings up another question that has so far been addressed only obliquely. Are all architectures Enterprise Architectures? Freshman Electrical Engineers are asked, Does electrical current from positive to negative or negative to positive?

The answer to both questions is, it all depends – on the position of the measuring device.

Chapter Four

IDEF Primer

We are drowning in information but starved for knowledge.
- JOHN NAISBITT

This chapter will focus on discussing how IDEF can fulfill the OV-5 and OV-7 and provide the business rules for OV-6a requirements for the DoDAF Architecture.

What is IDEF?
IDEF stands for Integrated DEFinition language. Created in the late 1970's, IDEF is a standard modeling technique for all US government agencies, and many private companies. It provides a common, public-domain language for modeling and describing processes, data, requirements, and functions.

The National Institute of Standards and Technology (NIST) announced its adoption of the IDEF0 and IDEF1X standards in 1993. IDEF0 and IDEF1X are listed in the Federal Information Processing Standards Publication (FIPS PUB) 183 and 184 respectively. The U.S. Department of Commerce, National Institute of Standards and Technology in Gaithersburg MD is the governing body for the FIPS Publications.

> The IDEFs are a true methodology. The FIPS documents tell precisely how to model, how to read models, the essence of good models and even how to form teams to build models.

IDEF is broken down into multiple components. This primer focuses on IDEF0 and IDEF1X as they can supply some of the required DoDAF views:

IDEF Level	What it does	DoDAF supported views	Answers the question:
IDEF0	Process Modeling	OV-5	What do I do?
IDEF1X	Data Modeling	OV-7	What do I need to know to do what I do?

Figure 4.1 IDEF Levels and DoDAF Views

IDEF0 Basics

An IDEF0 model has the following main characteristics:
- Context, Viewpoint, and Purpose
- Graphic Diagrams
    - Functions (Boxes)
    - ICOMs (Arrows)
    - Labels
- Glossary

The top level of an IDEF0 model is referred to as the A-0 level. An example follows:

Get a good IDEF0 A-0 with context, purpose, and viewpoint and you will have a good IDEF model. And the opposite is also true.

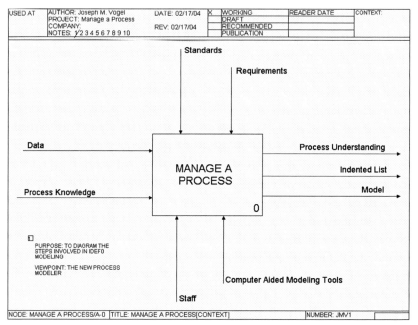

Figure 4.2 Example of A-0 Level

Context, Purpose, and Viewpoint
The A-0 level clearly shows the Context, Purpose, and Viewpoint. These directly correlate to the Context, Purpose, and Viewpoint on the DoDAF's AV-1 view.

Functions (Boxes)
Boxes represent functions that may be
- Activities
- Processes
- Operations
- Transformations

A function describes what happens in a particular environment. A function is regulated or triggered by at least one control.

ICOMs (Arrows)

An IDEF0 model has four types of arrows, which are also known as ICOMs. The table below provides a brief description of each one:

ICOMs	Name	Description
I	Input	A resource changed or consumed by the process (optional).
C	Control	A constraint on the operation of the process (mandatory).
O	Output	Something resulting from the process (mandatory).
M	Mechanism	Something that performs or enables the process, but is not consumed (optional).

Figure 4.3 Four ICOM Arrows in IDEF0 Model

Labels

Labels name functions, data, and objects. In the IDEF0 model, all boxes and arrows are labeled. Each label should be chosen to aid communication.

Function labels, located inside the function/activity box, are verb phrases. They should be the action of doing something such as 'Pay Bills' or 'Hire Employees.'

Arrow labels for the ICOMS, placed alongside or tied to the arrows, are nouns or noun phrases.

An IDEF0 Model is a graphic diagram with a text diagram for each graphic diagram and a glossary which contains the meaning of every Activity, Input, Output, Control, and Mechanism.

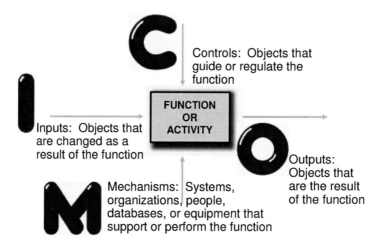

Figure 4.4 Summary of "ICOM" Acronym Meaning

Glossary

Every Activity, Input, Control, Output and Mechanism in the IDEF0 model must be in the glossary. This glossary can be shared between the IDEF0 and IDEF1X. Additionally, the glossary can act as the AV-2, Integrated Dictionary, a required DoDAF view.

Decomposition Hierarchy

IDEF0 Models are hierarchical in nature. They look at the function or process at its highest level, and then provide a view at each level below that.

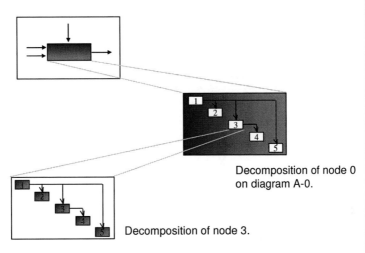

Figure 4.5 Example of Decomposition Hierarchy

Not only can the functions (represented as boxes on the diagram) be broken down into component parts, so can arrows. Arrows at higher levels can represent classes or categories of interfaces at lower levels. These can be classes of material interfaces or classes of information interfaces.

In this example, the mechanism Staff is broken down into 3 types of staff at lower levels: Users, DBA, and Programmers.

Reading the IDEF Model
Mechanisms act on Inputs subject to Controls in order to produce Outputs.

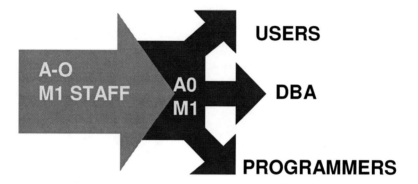

Figure 4.6 Example of 3-Level Mechanism

IDEF0 can support OV-5 and OV-6a
The OV-5, the Operational Activity Model, illustrates how the functions used in achieving a business goal. This view describes the demonstration of capabilities, operational activities, relationships among those activities, and inputs and outputs both internal and external to the enterprise architecture.

The IDEF0 model is one method of producing an acceptable OV-5. The functions from the IDEF0 model represent the operations. The ICOMs represent the inputs, outputs and relationships between the functions. Additionally, the IDEF0 model graphically represents the constraints on each activity within the model. Those constraints translate into the business rules and constraints required for the OV-6a, operation rules model, view.

IDEF1X Basics
IDEF1X stands for Integrated Definition for Data Modeling.

While IDEF0 is a representation of a functional model, IDEF1X is a representation of a data model. The main purpose of IDEF1X is to provide consistency in definitions and to support the creation of conceptual schemas.

Conceptual schemas must be:

1. Consistent within the infrastructure of the business.
2. Extendible so that adding new data does not require the redefinition of existing data.
3. Convertible to a user and data storage and access structures.

An IDEF1X model has the following four main characteristics:
- Entities – representations of things such as people, places, ideas, etc. - (Boxes)
- Relationships between things (Lines)
- Attributes - characteristics of things - (Attribute names within boxes)
- Keys – an attribute or multiple attributes that uniquely identifies an entity

An illustrative, but not complete, IDEF1X example model follows:

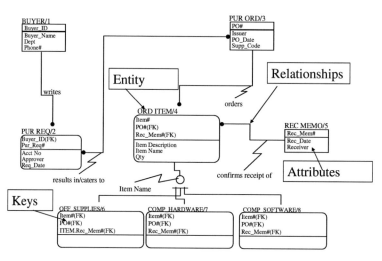

Figure 4.7 Example of IDEF1X Model

There are four phases to building an IDEF1X model.
1. Identify and describe entities (this can come from the DoDAF's AV-2).
2. Define relationships.
3. Define key attributes.
4. Define all other attributes.

Relationships are business rules with necessary specificity.

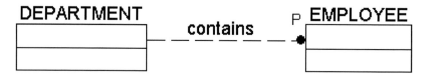

Figure 4.8 Example of a Relationship

This case specifies the business rule that a department contains one or more employees and that an employee is assigned to one department.

There are several types of relationship identifiers including the following:

- Non-Specific (Many to Many)
- Identifying (Specific)
- Non-identifying
- Category (Subtype)

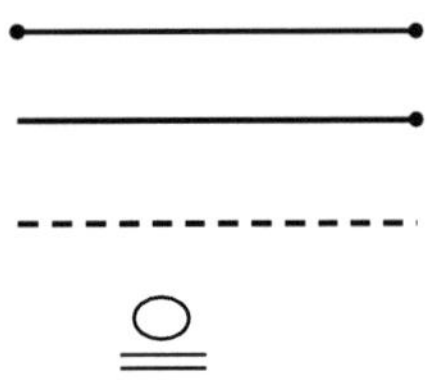

Figure 4.9 Types of Relationship Identifiers

Relationship Cardinality
Cardinality describes how many instances of one entity relate to an instance of another entity. Cardinality at the parent end of an identifying relationship is always 1. Symbols for cardinality are placed next to the dots on the child entity end of relationship lines.

(Blank)	=	0, 1 or more
P	=	1 or more
Z	=	0 or 1
N	=	n, where n is some whole number

Can IDEF1X support OV-7?

Absolutely!

The OV-7, the Logical Data Model, illustrates the architecture domain's system data types and entities as well as the relationships between them. The IDEF1X model satisfies the OV-7 view.

Chapter Five

UML Primer

Knowing is the measure of the man. By how much we know, so we are.
- RALPH WALDO EMERSON

What is the UML?

UML stands for the Unified Modeling Language. Don't forget the "the." Initiated in 1980 and promoted by three individuals who call themselves the 3 Amigos, UML is a modeling technique based on the object-oriented paradigm. The UML was created specifically for software designers who believe that Object Oriented databases have significant advantages over relational databases. UML is managed by the Object Management Group (OMG). There are over 30 books written about the UML. Unlike the IDEFs which are governed by FIPS, there is no UML standard. In fact, UML has interesting constructs such as abstraction and stereotyping that allow every UML to be different. While there is a "standard" symbology for UML diagrams, one well-known author says in his recent book that he changed his mind midway through the book and is not consistent.

This chapter is based on Sam's Teach Yourself UML in 24 Hours – 2nd Edition by Joseph Schmuller. This is the only reference found that is consistent across the UML diagram types. In many, many seminars there have been arguments

> The UML has no methodology.
>
> Proof of this assertion is that UML practitioners argue about this point.
>
> For this reason, we offer our own methodology connected to the DoDAF.

about what you are about to see. One seminar had 3 PhDs in Software Engineering. It seemed that the discussion was between three different sects of the same religion. What is presented here is consistent, if not complete and is used later in the DoDAF example project to build the DoDAF EA products.

As was said earlier, the UML is based upon objects. An object can be a person, place, thing or idea. (Nouns) Objects are often described in terms of their classification or (object class). An object class is a 'blueprint' of an object. An object class describes the anatomy of an object. Example:

> Objects are nouns – person, place or thing.

Objects exist in a class.

- Dennis Wisnosky exists in Object Class of Humans
    o Sub class Male
        ▪ Sub sub – etc. class, eventually gets to me, Dennis Wisnosky with certain Attributes able to perform certain Operations – All of this is my 'blueprint.'

Object Anatomy

- Name – A string used to identify a model element.
- Attribute – description of a named slot in a class. Each object of the class separator holds a value of the type.

- Operation – A specification of a transformation or query that an object may be called upon to execute.

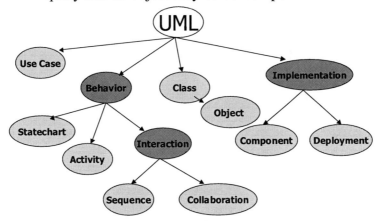

Figure 5.1 Typical UML diagrams and packages

The UML has 9 types of pre-defined diagrams and three packages.

How does the DoDAF use the UML?

DoDAF, and this is its biggest departure from C4ISR, uses the nine UML diagram types as the basis for, or as templates for 12 of its 26 products.

As stated above, there is no standard UML. And, there is no UML methodology. This UML Primer should be viewed as UML 101 on each diagram type. They are put together later in the "Minimalist Methodology." For now, one diagram type at a time is shown based on a standard syntax build, which is referred to as symbology built for each diagram type.

DoDAF says UCD is for OV-1, OV-4, OV-5 and SV-4

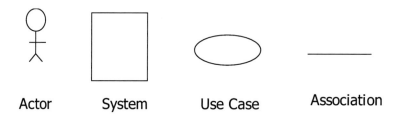

Figure 5.2 Use Case Symbology

The Use Case Diagram (UCD) purpose is to describe the functionality of a system in a horizontal way. UCDs have only 4 major elements: The **actors** that the system you are describing interacts with, the **system** itself, the **use cases**, or services, that the system knows how to perform, and the lines that represent **relationships** between these elements. The UCD is a top down activity model. While the DoDAF shows many actor symbols throughout, the purpose for the UCD is OK in OV-1, OV-4, and SV-4. But, best in OV-5.

Is there a UCD Standard?

There is no UCD standard equivalent to the IDEF FIPS. References abound. The UCD should be supported by a textual scenario. The scenario is a textual description of the meaning of the use case. In the Check Credit example below, there could be several scenarios. One could be for "Accepted Credit" and another of "Rejected Credit," for example. The high level UCD would look the same, but there would be two scenarios. It is critical that the EA Team agree on their standards for the UCD and the UCD Scenario.

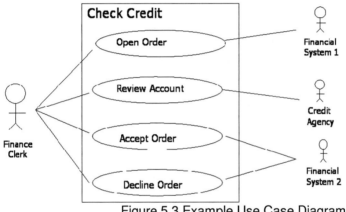

Figure 5.3 Example Use Case Diagram

Use text for multiple scenarios of your UCD

Can I use UML for Activity Models?

UML Activity Diagrams are used for the OV-5.

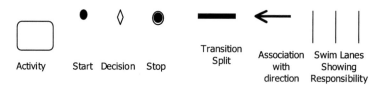

Figure 5.4 UML Activity Diagram Symbology

UML Activity Diagrams are also referred to as Swim Lane Diagrams or Rummler – Brache Diagrams. Alan Rummler and Gary Brache are 2 of the 3 amigos credited with the original UML. These diagrams are useful for describing responsibility and timing. In IDEF0, this responsibility is contained in the mechanisms. While these diagrams can be quite extensive, this diagram type is best used for small models.

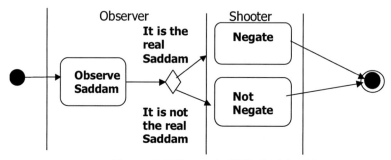

Figure 5.5 Example UML Activity Diagram

What do I do with my Objects?

Objects are primarily used in Class Diagrams. In the DoDAF OV-4, SV4 and SV-11 are all based on various forms of Class Diagrams. OV-7 is IDEF1X or Class.

The concept of Class in the Object was introduced in the discussion above. Class describes the structure of a system. Class can represent and structure information, products, documents, and organizations. Again, in the UML this may be viewed as a circular definition that includes additional words that must also be defined.

The information to build Class Diagrams is contained in the Activity Diagrams. Class diagrams describe the different types of objects that 'live' in a system and their relationships

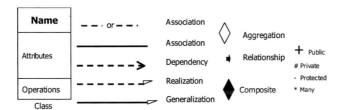

Figure 5.6 UML Class Diagram Symbology

The figure shows customer class with two sub classes.

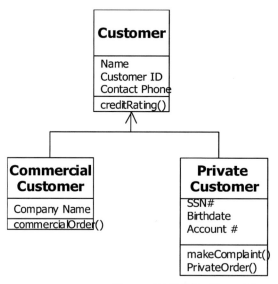

Figure 5.7 UML Class Diagram Example

Strange as it might seem, there is no information model in UML. Rather the information model is described as a 'specialization' of a class or an object diagram. The Minimalist Methodology uses IDEF1X for building the information model.

Where do UML State Diagrams fit into the DoDAF?

OV-6b and SV-10b use static State Diagrams. OV-6b recommends Simulation that requires information not contained in the State Diagram. The purpose of a State Diagram is to understand the behavior of objects with respect to one another. State Diagrams show the state of a single object.

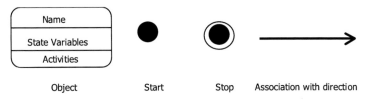

Figure 5.8 UML State Diagram Symbology

Labels may be placed on the Association. These labels may be trigger events containing messages transferred between the Objects.

Figure 5.9 UML State Diagram Example

Where Do Sequence Diagrams fit in?

While State Diagrams are specific to the state on an object, Sequence Diagrams show how objects communicate with one another over time.

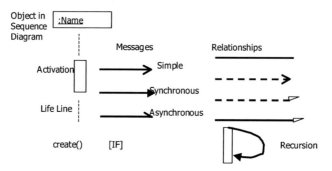

Figure 5.10 UML Sequence Diagram Symbology

Sequence Diagrams add life to the Activity Model. The information for Sequence Diagrams will be derived from what is learned in building the OV-5.

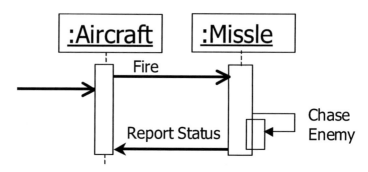

Figure 5.11 UML Sequence Diagram Example

Objects in Sequence Diagrams communicate through messages. These messages transfer control from one object to another. Each scenario of a Use Case will have a different Sequence Diagram.

How can I be sure organizations and systems collaborate?

The DoDAF uses UML Collaboration Diagrams for showing Operational Node Connectivity, the OV-2. Collaboration Diagrams are intended to show the complete collaboration between objects.

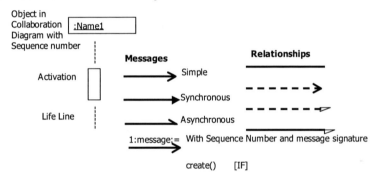

Figure 5.12 UML Collaboration Diagram Symbology

Collaboration Diagrams show how objects are statically connected. They are semantically equivalent to Sequence Diagrams, but emphasize context and organization of the objects, not the timing. Thus, they are arranged according to space, not to time.

In the example Collaboration Diagram, the aircraft sends the find foe message to the missile and gets a message back when the job is done.

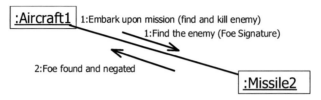

Figure 5.13 UML Collaboration Diagram Example

How are we really going to build a system?

The UML uses components to build systems. In the UML, software components are considered to be a physical part of the system -table, data file, executable code, .doc. The DoDAF **SV-1** System Interface Description is built from both Component Diagrams and Deployment Diagrams.

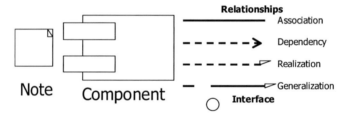

Figure 5.14 UML Component Diagram Symbology

Component Diagrams represent real world software.

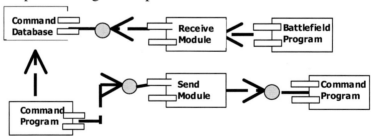

Figure 5.15 UML Component Diagram Example

UML Deployment Diagrams complete our UML Primer.

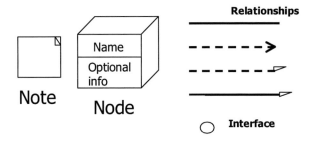

Figure 5.16 UML Deployment Diagram Symbology

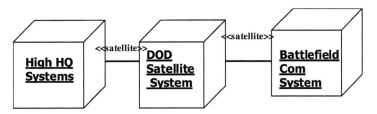

Figure 5.17 UML Deployment Diagram Symbology

In real life, UML Deployment Diagrams and Component Diagrams most often appear together because they are both necessary to fully describe a system. That is, each hardware node is shown with its embedded software.

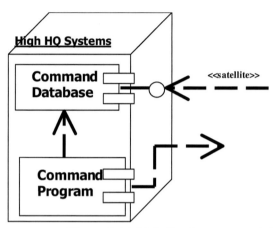

Figure 5.18 UML Deployment and Component Diagram Combined

Do I now know just enough about UML to be dangerous?

Absolutely! To begin with, this UML Primer is definitely for the Enterprise Architect, not the software engineer. DoDAF Wizdom takes the viewpoint of the operations person, not software designer, developer, or deliverer. It ignores some of the OO concepts dear to the hearts of UML aficionados such as inheritance. On the other hand, UML has wonderful concepts called Stereotypes and Abstractions. Use the symbology of this Primer and label your UML diagrams as Abstractions and you will build perfect UML modes every time. DoDAF volume II examples prove the point.

Chapter Six

Heading, Altitude and Air Speed
Time, Cost and Quality based KPIs

> *You've got to be very careful if you don't know where you're going, because you might not get there.*
> **- YOGI BERRA**

When the DoDAF talks about performance, it exclusively means technical performance in terms that promise that the right nodes talk and that they talk at the right time. The DoDAF uses Performance Parameters to measure such factors as Internodal Connectivity, Information Assurance, Timeliness, Periodicity and Security. The Operational Exchange Information Table OV-3 and the Systems Data Exchange Matrix (SV-6) DoDAF products are the realm of these Performance Parameters.

But, it has been shown that the DoDAF must be the basis for, or at least intersect with the OMB Business Reference Model and support the CCA Business Case.

How can this happen if the team does not gather supporting business based Performance Parameters? **It can't!**

Accordingly, this chapter focuses on how to build the business case. Before that, the chapter presents some DoDAF doctrine on Key Performance Parameters that

DoDAF contains little to help us build the business case.

technically support the Integrated Architecture, NCOW, and Born Joint concepts previously discussed.

For what purpose?

DoD is striving for outcomes. One of the latest buzzwords already known is Born Joint. Another buzzword is Maximum Organizational Effectiveness (MOE).

The Net-Centric Operations and Warfare (NCOW) Reference Model is intended to provide a common language and understanding of net-centricity and specify the core capabilities of a net-centric DoD architecture. An Integrated Architecture developed according to the DoDAF is supposed to define Operational Nodes, Organizational Relationships, Operational Activities, Systems Functions, Systems Data Exchange, and a Technical Architecture Profile.

What does this have to do with the DoDAF?

To define how to achieve interoperability, the DoDAF defines IERs (Information Exchange Requirements) which ride on "need lines" between the nodes of the Operational Node Connectivity (OV-2) products. The performance Parameters specific to each IER are included in the tables of the Operational Information Exchange Matrix (OV-3) and Systems Data Exchange Matrix (SV-6). These performance parameters are all that the DoDAF has to determine the MOE. But, the DoDAF only cares about technical performance, information assurance and security. The DoDAF does not care about the business performance discussed in Chapter 3.

Thus, a DoDAF EA could be massively technically described as to connectivity and contain nothing about the performance of the business. Further, in the C4ISR sense **every** node would be depicted on an OV-2 that **any** node could conceivably interact with. To resolve this dilemma, current thinking has gone in two directions and while that is being sorted out technically, DoDAF Wizdom strongly advocates a third.

What are the two directions DoD is taking to resolve this issue?

First: Performance Parameters are becoming Key Performance Parameters (KPPs). These are commonly 10% of all of the performance parameters.

Secondly: KPPs are becoming NR-KPPs (Net Ready – KPPs). They are typically thought of as being part of an Information Support Plan (ISP). Among other aspects, an ISP must document the program needs, dependencies, interface requirements, and incorporate the NR-KPPs. In attempting to move toward NR-KPP, the DoD has defined Key Interface Profiles (KIPs). KIPs define organizational boundaries, mission criticality, capability, interoperability, or efficiency issues.

Seventeen KIPs are to be developed. The Teleport KIP is the only one that has been completed as of this writing.

1. JTF to Coalition
2. Logical Networks to DISN Transport Backbone
3. Space to Terrestrial
4. TELEPORT
5. Client to Server
6. Application Server to Shared Data
7. DISN Service Delivery Node
8. Secure Enclave Service Delivery Node
9. JTF Component to JTF Headquarters
10. Application Server to Database Server
11. Joint Interconnection Service
12. Management System to Managed Systems
13. Application to COE/CCP (NCES/GES)
14. End System to PKI
15. Information Servers to IDM Infrastructure
16. IDM to Distribution Infrastructure
17. Management System to (integrated) Management Systems

What is the DoD Plan to have all of this resolved?

There are really two directions:

1) The move from node to node (1 to 1) to node to net (1 to net.)
2) Net Ready–Key Performance Parameters (NR-KPPs)

The reasons for these two directions should be clear, even if the paths to achieve them, are not.

First, node to node connectivity relies on the formula $N(N-1)$. This means that if 2 nodes are connected, there must be 2 paths, but if there are 10 connected nodes, there are 90 paths. If there are 100 connected nodes there are 900 paths and so on. One to net is exactly that – a node has one connection to the net and the net can connect any node to any other node.

Secondly: Net-Ready KPPS refer to "verifiable performance measures and associated metrics required to evaluate the timely, accurate, and complete exchange and use of information to satisfy information needs for a given capability."

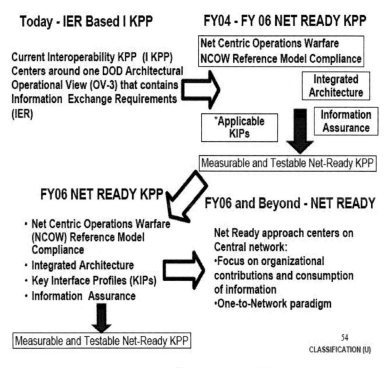

Figure 6.1 N-KPP plan

"The NR-KPP is comprised of the following elements:

Compliance with the NCOW RM.

Compliance with applicable GIG Key Interface Profiles.

Verification of compliance with DoD information assurance requirements.

Supporting integrated architecture products required to assess information exchange and use for a given capability."

DoD has sort of a plan for achieving NR-KPPs, as shown in the figure, for FY2006 and beyond. But, there are more "known unknowns" than "known knowns" at this time.

This is not so in the world of Key Performance Indicators (KPIs) for measuring business goodness – the problem is the opposite, there are too many "knowns." One indicator says one thing and another says something else or nothing at all. While there are models and charts to follow, each must be interpreted and compared to others. The bewildering array of inputs causes managers to feel "No one really knows what is going on here!" and "Where to fit in the value chain anyway?" "All of it is just too complex!"

Clinger Cohen is all about Asset Management. In the book BPR Wizdom flying an aircraft was used as an example of extreme asset management. This example is repeated here greatly simplified. The detail is in BPR Wizdom.

How do Aircraft Pilots Manage Their Assets?

Look into the cockpit of today's airliners. There are a bewildering number of displays, buttons, knobs, dials, levers, switches, circuit breakers, and in some airliners, two control wheels. But how are Airbuses steered? They have sticks, not control wheels. How do pilots look at all of those instruments and manage the assets being displayed? The answer is that the pilot does not need to know everything about every asset.

How do pilots perform asset management? First, many of the systems are automatic. They only report when something goes wrong. Even then, there are considerable backup systems built in, known as redundancy, to automatically take over in an emergency, or they can be switched to by the pilot. Radios, vacuum pumps and alternators, for example, are always redundant. That is, there are at least two of them in a complex aircraft.

But what if something goes wrong that a system cannot fix? What then?

"**24 August 2001; Air Transit A330-200; near the Azores Islands, Portugal:** The aircraft was cruising across the Atlantic at 39,000 feet (11,900 meters) on a flight from Toronto to Lisbon when the right engine lost power. The left engine quit about 13 minutes later. Both engines lost power as a result of fuel starvation. There had been a leak in the fuel system near the right engine, and an open crossfeed valve allowed fuel to be lost from both wing tanks. The leak had been noticed by the crew about an hour prior to the engines shutting down, and the aircraft was already diverting toward Lajes military airfield in the

Pilots only need 3 Performance Indicators.

Azores. After the last engine lost power, the crew was able to glide for 20 minutes for about 115 miles (185 km) to Lajes airfield and avert a mid-ocean ditching"

In this situation, the pilot relies on what he/she was taught in very basic training. Forget about everything else. There are only three necessary assets: ***heading, altitude, and air speed***.

Of all the asset indicators in the cockpit, these are the only three that are important. They are used exactly the same way in a Sports Aircraft as they are used in a Boeing 747.

Heading is the indicator that tells the pilot the direction the airplane is going. Heading is indicated by the directional gyro or the compass. Heading also answers the question "is the airplane going straight, or is it turning?"

Altitude is the indicator that shows how high the aircraft is above the ground. Altitude is indicated on an altimeter. The altimeter also tells the pilot if the aircraft is descending or climbing and at what rate.

Airspeed is the indicator that tells the pilot if the aircraft is going too fast or too slow. The airspeed indicator helps the pilot to stay in the operating safety envelope of that particular aircraft. The aircraft stalls if it goes too slow, or may breakup or become uncontrollable if it goes to fast. The job of the pilot is to keep the airspeed indicator in the "Green Arc."

Does the pilot really need 3 Performance Indicators?

Yes! The pilot needs three, not one or two. More than three is superfluous information. The pilot performs an instrument scan and verifies that each indicator is telling the truth by comparing one to another. If all three together do not make sense, the pilot believes the two that agree.
For example in straight and level flight, nothing should be changing. If the airspeed indicator says that the aircraft is suddenly going faster, and the pilot has not added power, then the only conclusion is that the aircraft is descending. If the altimeter indicates a steady altitude and the heading indicator has not moved, then the airspeed indicator is broken. Inversely, if the altimeter indicates a climb or a descent, then the airspeed indicator must also move. If it does not, then the pilot looks at the heading indicator. If it is steady, then the altitude indicator is lying.

In the real world example above, all the pilots had was their skill and indicators of heading, altitude and airspeed. For the DoDAF business case the equivalent must be constructed. Pilots are taught to believe their instruments. They are also taught to always crosscheck any two instruments with a third. Sailors, who need only a watch and compass to navigate, are taught to always have three watches, the two that agree are correct. When the complexities of flying are reduced to managing only three assets, pilots and their passengers are not in danger and can enjoy the experience. The complexities of business are reduced to the only three necessary asset indicators. Our

> Heading, altitude and airspeed is time, cost and quality.

heading, altitude and airspeed equivalents for the DoDAF CCA business case are Time, Cost and Quality. This will be our Key Performance Indicators.

DoDAF and Business Process Reengineering have many parallels to this flying scenario. BPR seeks to reduce the complexities of business asset management by building business process models, analyzing the properties of these models, exercising these models in what-if scenarios and so on. Enterprise Architecture and BPR Projects are a careful mix of humans and technology. A pilot must know his or her plane like an enterprise architect must know his or her organization. Included in this knowledge is a deep understanding of the organization's assets, both those of the machine *(tangible assets)* and those of the pilot *(intangible assets)*.

> Enterprise Architects must know their organization.

How are Time, Cost and Quality linked to the business of the organization through the DoDAF?

DoDAF provides the easy answer. The answer is in the OV-5, the Operational Activity Model. DoDAF says, "To a very large extent, **OV-5** provides the foundation for the remaining OV products. Therefore, a reasonably stable version of **OV-5** should be developed before the other products are started."

DoDAF is right on the money on this point. Business is all about operations. The "Operational Activity Model" is the model that describes what the business does. It is the flight plan of the business. It only makes sense that understanding the KPIs of the business is necessary to understand the business.

The OV-5 is an activity model of the type that BPR practitioners build as a mainstay of business process analysis. As was said previously, the DoDAF identifies three choices for building these models.

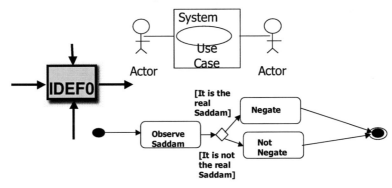

Figure 6.2 OV-5 Operational Activity Modeling Methods

IDEF0 is the best choice for working with the Enterprise Architecture KPIs. There are many reasons, but the primary reason is because IDEF0 has two alternate views.

Chapter 4 showed IDEF0 Activity Models in the form of graphic diagrams of boxes and arrows. Under the set of diagrams that is the model is the indented list. The Indented list view facilitates analysis of the AS-IS, performing what if analysis of alternative TO-BE scenarios. The Node Tree view facilitates creation of the operations flow model for both AS-IS understanding and TO-BE reorganization.

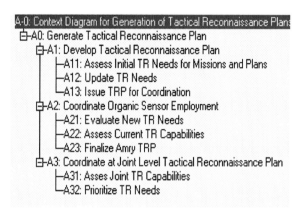

Figure 6.3 IDEF0 Indented List

As shown below, the indented list carries the KPIs of Time, Cost and Quality. And it serves as the basis for the business case that can be as simple or as complicated as necessary to get what the customer wants.

The example shown here is a simple spread sheet that can show the results of the analysis. In reality, the analysis is performed using the approach accepted by the customer.

Activity Based Costing (ABC) is the most commonly accepted approach for doing a cost analysis.

Creating a Time Line or a Gantt chart with Microsoft Project could be the basis for analysis looking for bottlenecks or to determine activities that could be performed in parallel.

Quality analysis is perhaps more subjective, but what works every time is a voice of the customer technique such as TQM.

ACTIVITY	COST	CYCLE TIME	RUN TIME	Quality
A0:Generate Tactical Reconnaissance Plan	$101,050			
A1:Develop Tactical Reconnaissance Plan	$35,317.50			
A11:Assess Initial TR Needs for Missions and Plans	$15,102.50	200d	100d	
A12:Update TR Needs	$10,152.50	50d	5d	
A13:Issue TRP for Coordination	$10,062.50	25d	10d	
A2:Coordinate Organic Sensor Employment	$55,475			
A21:Evaluate New TR Needs	$30,170	200d	25d	
A22:Assess Current TR Capabilities	$20,137.50	100d	50d	
A23:Finalize Amry TRP	$5,167.50	10d	5d	
A3:Coordinate at Joint Level Tactical Reconnaissance Plan	$10,257.50			
A31:Asses Joint TR Capabilities	$5,175	100d	50d	
A32:Prioritize TR Needs	$5,082.50	10d	5d	

Figure 6.4 KPI Analysis by Activity

The Activity List is the anchor for all analysis.

Various products and tools can be used to perform this analysis. The Wizdom product performs Time analysis with MS Project often supplemented with Visio, the ABC analysis with MS Excel and custom macros and the Quality analysis depending upon the needs of the customer. Examples follow. Each is based on the IDEF0 Activity list with appended Time, Cost and Quality Properties. This data is automatically exported to the appropriate tool for the analysis and then imported back into the Activity list that is the heart of the IDEF0 Model. Shown below is the basis for a time line analysis. The goal is to minimize cycle time by maximizing the percentage of run time to perform each activity. The analyst iterates through AS-IS and TO-BE scenarios until optimal is achieved.

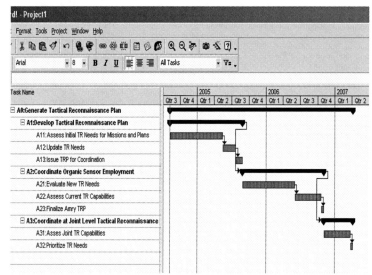

Figure 6.5 Time Analysis with MS Project

As with the Cost and Quality Indicators, there is a Time Performance Indicator associated with each activity in the IDEF0 Diagram beginning with the lowest level Activities. The Indicator values are rolled up from the bottom to get the total cost or benefit of the Operation.

The Time Indicators exported to MS Project and displays the picture above. Changes made go back to the IDEF0 model and to the final analysis spread sheet, which was shown in Figure 6.4. An example of the indicator Table that is used is shown below with Time, Cost and Organization shown for the children of the IDEF0 A2 Node.

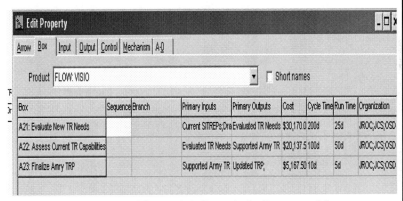

Figure 6.6 Sample Indicators table

Cost Analysis is performed using classical ABC. First: Cost Elements and Organizations are identified. Time spent in performing each Activity is captured in a table at the level of detail required in each organization. Again, this begins with the lowest level Activities and all numbers are rolled up automatically. Without the Activity List, this could not be done.

Second: A table of organization expenditure by cost element is established. This information is available from the organization's traditional budgeting process.

Third: The cost analysis output is the cross product of these two tables. It is the cost-by-cost element for each Activity.

ABC COST ANALYSIS OUTPUT   (In Millions of Dollars)

FUNCTIONS	Oversight	GS Labor	Mil Labor	TOTAL
A0:Generate Tactical Reconnaissance Plan	100600	200	250	101050
A1:Develop Tactical Reconnaissance Plan	35190	60	67.5	35317.5
A11:Assess Initial TR Needs for Missions and Plans	15055	22.5	25	15102.5
A12:Update TR Needs	10105	22.5	25	10152.5
A13:Issue TRP for Coordination	10030	15	17.5	10062.5
A2:Coordinate Organic Sensor Employment	55250	100	125	55475
A21:Evaluate New TR Needs	30070	45	55	30170
A22:Assess Current TR Capabilities	20065	32.5	40	20137.5
A23:Finalize Amry TRP	5115	22.5	30	5167.5
A3:Coordinate at Joint Level Tactical Reconnaissance Plan	10160	40	57.5	10257.5
A31:Asses Joint TR Capabilities	5105	27.5	42.5	5175
A32:Prioritize TR Needs	5055	12.5	15	5082.5

Figure 6.7 Cross Product showing true labor by activity

What does this type of analysis tell us? In this case, Oversight is by far the biggest cost and Planning and Evaluation cost much more than doing. But, it is a must to check the findings from Time – Figure 6.5 and Cost – Figure 6.7 against our Quality Indicators. As stated earlier, the Third KPI is Quality. Here it is up to the project team. Approaches used range from a very formal "House of Quality" or a table in which individual responsible for each activity, the mechanisms of the IDEF0 Model simply rank the affect of that activity on quality of the output from that activity.

And as the icing on the cake for the CCA Business Case, the IDEF0 Model is used with the embedded KPIs to build a Swim lane Diagram. This is another OV-5 construct. In the minimalist methodology it is useful to get us ready to do a simulation a.k.a. OV-6b.

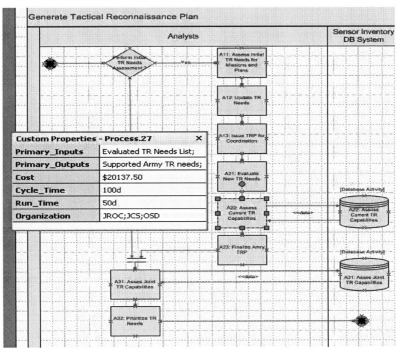

Figure 6.8 OV-5 Swim Lane Diagram with example KPI

This diagram is an MS Visio representation with the KPIs extracted for the A22 node. It was initiated automatically with the KPIs transferred, and then alternatives were developed in Visio.

What was the source of the Model we just examined?

The analysis example above is from the DoD test of a CADM compliant OV-5 file from the DoDAF Architecture Repository System.

Is the example we saw the only way to do DoDAF Business Case Analysis?

Absolutely not! But, works. It uses off-the-shelf de facto or de jour standards and is based on IDEF0, the only FIPS-compliant Operations Activity Modeling Methodology. The reader is expected to greatly improve upon this approach. But, do it this way, and you will feel like you are flying through CAVU weather.

Chapter Seven

DoDAF Products Unmasked

The unit within the system with the most behavioral responses available to it controls the system

- FIRST LAW OF CYBERNETICS

It has been shown that there are 26 DoDAF products and that for all practical purposes the team must build at least 15 of them. This chapter shows that both the IDEFs and UML will be used to build all but a text document, the AV-1, and the products that are tables.

In DoDAF Volume II, DoDAF products are each described using a standard nomenclature. The description begins with Product Definition, then Product Purpose, then Product Detailed Description. Then the description moves on to include statements such as UML or IDEF applicability and in some case example products are shown that are sometimes labeled as notional. Finally, there is a CADM ER model of the product.

DoDAF Wizdom takes the position that the most relevant information is the statement of purpose. After this, much is left to the interpretation of the writer and of the reader. Therefore, DoDAF Wizdom quotes Purpose, Definition and a partial Detailed Description for each of the 26 products. There is a notation for the products essential to Wizdom's minimalist methodology introduced in the next chapter.

Smiley face is our Minimalist Notation for necessary products for DoDAF "Wizdom," for integrated architecure, 6212.01 and NCOW.

We use a single fictitious military example to show all 26 DoDAF products.

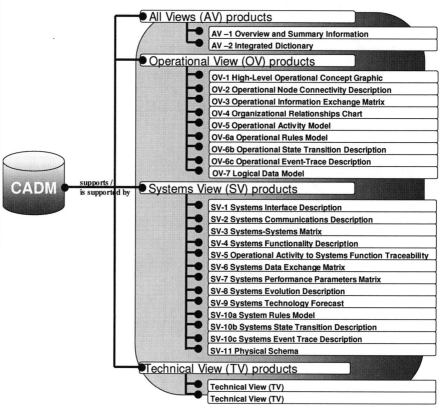

Figure 7.1 DoDAF Products and CADM

How do I set the context purpose and Viewpoint of my project?

Follow the template of the AV-1 and you can't go wrong. Every DoDAF project that the authors have seen has used the AV-1 right out of the box in a simple Word document.

Overview and Summary Information (AV-1)
Product Purpose. "AV-1 contains sufficient textual information to enable a reader to select one architecture from among many to read in more detail. AV-1 serves two additional purposes. In the initial phases of architecture development, it serves as a planning guide. Upon completion of an architecture, AV-1 provides summary textual information concerning the architecture."

AV-1 lives for the life of the project. Its Context, purpose and viewpoint must match that of the OV-5.

Product Definition.
"The Overview and Summary Information provides executive-level summary information in a consistent form that allows quick reference and comparison among architectures. AV-1 includes assumptions, constraints, and limitations that may affect high-level decision processes involving the architecture."

Product Detailed Description.
"The AV-1 product comprises a textual executive summary of a given architecture"

The AV-1 contains a textual summary of management information necessary to understand the Architecture including its intended use and its builders.

AV-1 is always a Word document matching the following template.

Use exactly this for your AV-1.

- **Architecture Project Identification**
  - Name
  - Architect
  - Organization Developing the Architecture
  - Assumptions and Constraints
  - Approval Authority
  - Date Completed
  - Level of Effort and Projected and Actual Costs to Develop the Architecture

- **Scope: Architecture View(s) and Products Identification**
  - Views and Products Developed
  - Time Frames Addressed
  - Organizations Involved

- **Purpose and Viewpoint**
  - Purpose, Analysis, Questions to be Answered by Analysis of the Architecture
  - From Whose Viewpoint the Architecture is Developed

- **Context**
  - Mission – Doctrine, Goals, and Vision
  - Rules, Criteria, and Conventions Followed
  - Tasking for Architecture Project and Linkages to Other Architectures

- **Tools and File Formats Used • Findings**
  - Analysis Results
  - Recommendations

Figure 7.2 AV-1 Template

AV-1 can be viewed essentially as a form to be filled out. You will see in our minimalist methodology that it lasts for the life of the EA project.

Architecture Project Identification		
• Name		PROJECT LITTLE EYE
• Architect		WIZDOM SYSTEMS INC.
• Organization Developing the Architecture		US ARMY
• Assumptions and Constraints		Constraint: Budget: $7.8 Million, less than 1 year to complete.
• Approval Authori ty		OMB
• Date Completed		(In process)
Scope: Architecture View(s) and Products Identification		
• Views and Products Developed		(OV1), (OV2), (OV4), (OV5), (OV6b) (OV6c), (OV7), (SV1), (SV4), (SV10b), (S
• Time Frames Addressed		Jan 2 04 –Mar. 2 04: (OV1), (OV2), (OV4), (OV5), (OV6b) Mar 2 04 – May 2 04: (OV6c), (OV7), (SV1), (SV4), May 2 04 – Jul 2 04: (SV10b), (SV10c), (SV11)
• Organizations Involved		US AIRFORCE, WIZDOM SYSTEMS INC., US ARMY
Purpose and Viewpoint		
• Purpose, Analysis, Questions to be answered by Analysis of the Architecture		Project Purpose: To understand the leadership situation in the battlefield and a systems necessary to improve the effectiveness of leadership. Analysis: Will review the views necessary to accomplish the pject's purpose. Questions: Can UAVs deliver quality leadership to troops in the field?
• From Whose Viewpoint the Architecture is Developed		Viewpoint is from the Battlefield Commanders
Context		
• Mission		Mission: To provide on-time leadership to troops in the field.
• Doctrine, Goals, and Vision		Goals: *Provide distribution of raw and processed data from a new tactical UAV to sup spanning the joint task force to platoon levels
• Rules, Criteria, and Conventions Followed		Rules: *Platoons donot have to receive raw data directly, verbal commands are sufficie *Requested information from a platoon must be answered, if at all possible, with minutes of the request, preferably within seconds of most requests
• Tasking for Architecture Pr oject Linkages to Other Architectures		Tasks: <See Microsoft Project LITTLEYE.mpd>
Tools and File Formats Used:		
Findings		
• Analysis Results		<In Process>
• Recommendations		<In Process>

Figure 7.3 AV-1 for our common example

Integrated Dictionary (AV-2)

Product Purpose. "AV-2 provides a central repository for a given architecture's data and metadata. AV-2 enables the set of architecture products to stand alone, allowing them to be read and understood with minimal reference to outside resources. AV-2 is an accompanying reference to other products, and its value lies in unambiguous definitions. The key to long-term interoperability can reside in the accuracy and clarity of these definitions." Many Architects view the AV-2 as the most valuable DoDAF product. For the very first time true understanding of the As-Is can be achieved because each term is defined in context.

Product Definition. "The Integrated Dictionary contains definitions of terms used in the given architecture. It consists of textual definitions in the form of a glossary, a repository of architecture data, their taxonomies, and their metadata (i.e., data about architecture data), including metadata for tailored products, associated with the architecture products developed. Metadata are the architecture data types, possibly expressed in the form of a physical schema. In this document, architecture data types are referred to as architecture data elements."

Product Detailed Description. "AV-2 defines terms used in an architecture, but it is more than a simple glossary. Many architectural products have implicit or explicit information in the form of a glossary, a repository of architecture data, their taxonomies, and their metadata. Each labeled item (e.g., icon, box, or connecting line) in the graphical representation has a corresponding entry in AV-2. Each item from a textual representation of an architectural product also has a corresponding entry in AV-2."

There is no UML or IDEF representation for AV-2. However, virtually every tool has the ability to build a glossary or dictionary containing every term in the model. Architects are strongly encouraged to use this utility. Choose the one from the most used tool and maintain the glossary current.

Figure 7.4 AV-2 for our common example

"Operational Views (OV) describes the tasks and activities, operational elements, and information exchanges required to conduct operations."

High-Level Operational Concept Graphic (OV-1)

Product Purpose. "The purpose of OV-1 is to provide a quick, high-level description of what the architecture is

Use the glossary of your most common tool for your AV-2.

supposed to do, and how it is supposed to do it. This product can be used to orient and focus detailed discussions. Its main utility is as a facilitator of human communication, and it is intended for presentation to high-level decision makers."

Strange as it may seem, OV-1 as an essential product went away when the DoDAF replaced the C4ISR Framework Architecture, but it is included in our minimal list.

Product Definition. "The High-Level Operational Concept Graphic describes a mission and highlights main operational nodes (see OV-2 definition) and interesting or unique aspects of operations. It provides a description of the interactions between the subject architecture and its environment, and between the architecture and external systems. A textual description accompanying the graphic is crucial. Graphics alone are not sufficient for capturing the necessary architecture data."

Product Detailed Description. "OV-1 consists of a graphical executive summary for a given architecture with accompanying text. The product identifies the mission/domain covered in the architecture and the viewpoint reflected in the architecture. OV-1 should convey, in simple terms, what the architecture is about and an idea of the players and operations involved. The content of OV-1 depends on the scope and intent of the architecture, but in general it describes the business processes or missions, high-level operations, organizations,

OV-1 is a High-level Graphic

and geographical distribution of assets. The product should frame the operational concept (what happens, who does what, in what order, to accomplish what goal) and highlight interactions to the environment and other external systems."

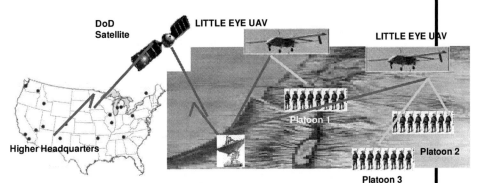

Figure 7.5 OV-1 Example

OV-1 is always a graphic. It may be supported by text. There can be no wrong OV-1.

Operational Node Connectivity Description (OV-2)

Product Purpose. "OV-2 is intended to track the need to exchange information from specific operational nodes (that play a key role in the architecture) to others. OV-2 does not depict the connectivity between the nodes."

The lock on the OV-2 is agreeing upon the need to exchange information.

Product Definition. "The Operational Node Connectivity Description graphically depicts the operational nodes (or organizations) with needlines between those nodes that indicate a need to exchange information. The graphic includes internal operational nodes (internal to the architecture) as well as external nodes."

Product Detailed Description. "The main features of this product are the operational nodes and the needlines between them that indicate a need to exchange information. The product indicates the key players and the interactions necessary to conduct the corresponding operational activities of OV-5."

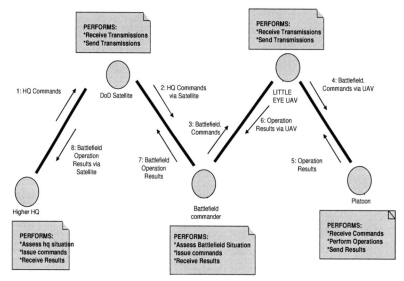

Figure 7.6 OV-2 Operational Node Connectivity

The DoDAF shows a UML Use Case notation for OV-2, but this has not been seen in practice.

Operational Information Exchange Matrix (OV-3)

Product Purpose. "Information exchanges express the relationship across the three basic architecture data elements of an OV (operational activities, operational nodes, and information flow) with a focus on the specific aspects of the information flow and the information content. Certain aspects of the information exchange can be crucial to the operational mission and should be tracked as attributes in OV-3. For example, if the subject architecture concerns tactical battlefield targeting, then the timeliness of the enemy target information is a significant attribute of the information exchange."

Product Definition. "The Operational Information Exchange Matrix details information exchanges and identifies *"who* exchanges *what* information, with *whom, why* the information is necessary, and *how* the information exchange must occur." [CJCSI 6212.01B, 2000] There is not a one-to-one mapping of OV-3 information exchanges to OV-2 needlines; rather, many individual information exchanges may be associated with one needline."

Product Detailed Description. "OV-3 identifies information elements and relevant attributes of the information exchange and associates the exchange to the producing and consuming operational nodes and activities and to the needline that the exchange satisfies."

OV-3 is a table containing **Information Exchange Identifiers** (IERS) and their characteristics in terms of:
- IER Information Element Description
- Producer
- Consumer
- Nature of Transaction
- Performance Attributes
- Information Assurance
- Security

Need line	Info Ex ID	Mission / Scenario	Trigger Event	Timeliness	Sending OP Node	Receiving OP Node
HQ Commands	1	ASSESS SITUATION	Upon arrival of field info	Immediate	Higher HQ	DoD Satellite
HQ Commands Via Satellite	2	ASSESS SITUATION	upon result arrival	JIT	DoD Satellite	Battlefield Commander
Battlefield Commands	3	ASSESS SITUATION	Upon result arrival	JIT	Battlefield Commander	Little Eye
Battlefield Commands via Little Eye UAV	4	SEND COMMANDS	Upon command arrival	Immediate	Little Eye	Platoon
Operation Results	5	RECEIVE COMMANDS	Upon command arrival	Immediate	Platoon	Little Eye
Operation Results Via Little Eye UAV	6	PERFORM OPERATION	Upon command arrival	Immediate	Little Eye	Battlefield Commander
Battlefield Operation Results	7	SEND RESULTS	Upon Operation Completion	Immediate	Battlefield Commander	DoD Satellite
Battlefield Operation Results Via Satellite	8	SEND RESULTS	Upon Operation Completion	Immediate	DoD Satellite	Higher HQ

Figure 7.7 OV-3

It is DoD's goal that IERs will be replaced by the one to net concept as mentioned previously.

Organizational Relationships Chart (OV-4)
Product Purpose. "This product clarifies the various relationships that can exist between organizations and sub-organizations within the architecture and between internal and external organizations."

Product Definition. "The Organizational Relationships Chart illustrates the command structure or relationships (as opposed to relationships with respect to a business process flow) among human roles, organizations, or organization types that are the key players in an architecture."

Product Detailed Description. "OV-4 illustrates the relationships among organizations or resources in an architecture. These relationships can include supervisory reporting, command and control relationships, and command-subordinate relationships. Another type of relationship is a coordination relationship between equals, where two organizations coordinate or collaborate without one having a supervisory or command relationship over the other. Others may be defined depending on the purpose of the architecture. Architects should feel free to define any kinds of relationships necessary and important within their architecture to support the goals of the architecture. For example, dynamic teams or task forces (i.e., new operational nodes) may be created in real time with only limited life spans and assigned missions, and could have needlines assigned to them. The creating node and the created node have a unique relationship that should be documented."

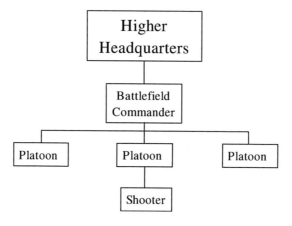

Figure 7.8 OV-4

Operational Activity Model (OV-5)
Product Purpose. OV-5 can be used to:

> "• Clearly delineate lines of responsibility for activities when coupled with OV-2
> • Uncover unnecessary operational activity redundancy
> • Make decisions about streamlining, combining, or omitting activities
> • Define or flag issues, opportunities, or operational activities and their interactions (information flows among the activities) that need to be scrutinized further
> • Provide a necessary foundation for depicting activity sequencing and timing in OV-6a, OV-6b, and OV-6c"

Reading the first three bullets above brings us back to the original goals of IDEF0 in FIPS 183. The goals are the same for an IDEF0 model.

Product Definition. "The Operational Activity Model describes the operations that are normally conducted in the course of achieving a mission or a business goal. It describes capabilities, operational activities (or tasks), input and output (I/O) flows between activities, and I/O flows to/from activities that are outside the scope of the architecture. High-level operational activities should trace to (are decompositions of) a Business Area, an Internal Line of Business, and/or a Business Sub-Function as published in OMB's Business Reference."

Product Detailed Description. "OV-5 describes capabilities, operational activities (or tasks), I/O flows between activities, and I/O flows to/from activities that are outside the scope of the architecture."

DoDAF offers three choices for the OV-5: Use Case, UML Activity Models and IDEF0. In addition, DoDAF offers sage advice of two types:

"After the **Operational Activity Model (OV-5)** is developed" "The products are each dependent on **OV-5** but not on each other." And, "To a very large extent, **OV-5** provides the foundation for the remaining OV products. Therefore, a reasonably stable version of **OV-5** should be developed before the other products are started."

DoDAF Wizdom also believes that the OV-5 is the key to successful DoDAF architecture projects.

What are the three OV-5 choices?

The choices are UML Use Case and Activity Models from the UML and IDEF0. Examples of these models were shown in previous chapters. This chapter has real models. First, a little personal bias based upon years of experience:

CONCENTRATE ON IDEF0

IDEF0 has many, many benefits. IDEF0 contains all that is needed for many other DoDAF products and, as was shown earlier, provides the basis for the CCA business case.

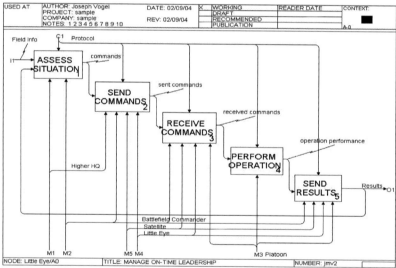

Figure 7.9 OV-5 IDEF0 Operations Activity Model

One of the benefits is that with some tools, the user can literally push a button and get the corresponding Use Case and a head start on a Rummler Brache Swim Lane Diagram.

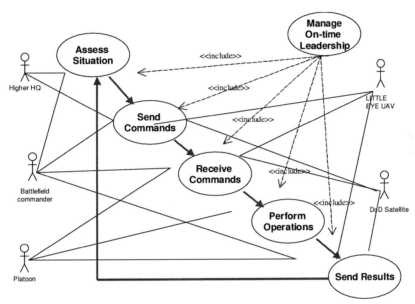

Figure 7.10 OV-5 Use Case Operations Activity Model

This example was literally produced by Wizdom Process*Works!* with a single button push. Because IDEF0 does not consider flow, this was added to the Use Case Diagram. Approached in this manner, a change in IDEF0 automatically becomes a change in the Use Case.

Go directly to Swim Lane Diagrams using the sequence properties discussed earlier in Chapter 6 to use Process Flow as part of the Business Case Analysis.

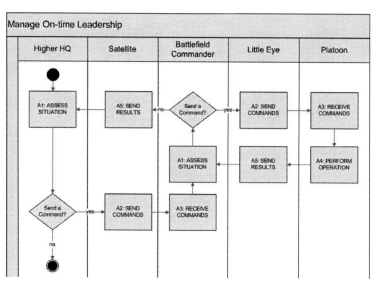

Figure 7.11 OV-5 UML Operations Activity Model

To produce this diagram, the IDEF0 diagram was exported to Visio where the details that IDEF0 is not aware of were added.

The IDEF0 Text Diagram and the Use Case Scenario are not shown here. It is suggested that they be the same – thus, they are absolutely associated with the correct IDEF0 Diagram and there is 100% uniformity with the AV-2.

What else comes from the IDEF0?

Depending on the rules that the team sets up, much is contained in the mechanisms. They include the organizations for OV-4, the systems for virtually every SV, the nodes of OV-2 and more.

Operational Activity Sequence and Timing Descriptions OV-6A, 6B and 6C

The OV-6's for Business Operations and the SV-10's for systems is as close as the DoDAF gets in helping us to describe the dynamics of an organization.

Operational Rules Model (OV-6a)

Product Purpose. "At a top level, rules should at least embody the concepts of operations defined in OV-1 and should provide guidelines for the development and definition of more detailed rules and behavioral definitions that will occur later in the architecture definition process."

Product Definition. "The Operational Rules Model specifies operational or business rules are constraints on an enterprise, a mission, an operation, a business, or an architecture. While other OV products (e.g., OV-1, OV-2, and OV-5) describe the structure of a business—what the business can do—for the most part, they do not describe what the business *must* do, or what it *cannot* do. At the mission level, OV-6a may consist of doctrine, guidance, rules of engagement, and so forth. At the operation level, rules may include such things as a military Operational Plan (OPLAN). At lower levels, OV-6a describes the rules under which the architecture or its nodes behave under specified conditions. Such rules can be expressed in a textual form, for example, 'If (these conditions) exist, and (this event) occurs, then (perform these actions).'"

Product Detailed Description. *"Rules are statements that define or constrain some aspect of the mission, or the architecture.* It is intended to assert operational structure or to control or influence the mission thread. As the product name implies, the rules captured in OV-6a are operational (i.e., mission-oriented) not systems-oriented. These rules can include such guidance as the conditions under which operational control passes from one entity to another or the conditions under which a human role is authorized to proceed."

These business rules are in text. If IDEF1X is used for the OV-7, then they are virtually automatic. Here is an example:

In the IDEF0 Diagram above for Manage On Time Leadership, there are 5 Activities: Assess Situation, Send Commands, Receive Commands, Perform Operation, and Receive Results. The corresponding IDEF1X data model will be shown in the next section. It will show the relationships between the entities performing these operations and the underlying business rules within which they operate.

With this example, the OV-6A would include:

> **OPERATIONAL RULES:**
> 1) "A new Operation cannot be performed before the results of a previous operation are known unless 24 hours have passed with no to assess the situation."
>
> 2) "Higher Headquarters issue commands to Battlefield Commander
>
> 3) "Battlefield Commanders issue commands to Platoons."
>
> 4) "Platoons carry out Operations and report results to Battlefield Commanders."
>
> 5) "Battlefield Commanders report results to Higher Headquarters."

Figure 7.12 OV-6A Operational Rules Model

Operational State Transition Description (OV-6b)

Product Purpose. "The explicit sequencing of activities in response to external and internal events is not fully expressed in OV-5. An Operational State Transition Description can be used to describe the explicit sequencing of the operational activities. Alternatively, OV-6b can be used to reflect the explicit sequencing of actions internal to a single operational activity or the sequencing of operational activities with respect to a specific operational node."

Product Definition. "The Operational State Transition Description is a graphical method of describing how an operational node or activity responds to various events by changing its state. The diagram represents the sets of events to which the architecture will respond (by taking an action to move to a new state) as a function of its current state. Each transition specifies an event and an action."

Product Detailed Description. "OV-6b is based on the statechart diagram. A state machine is defined as "a specification that describes all possible behaviors of some dynamic model element. Behavior is modeled as a traversal of a graph of state nodes interconnected by one or more joined transition arcs that are triggered by the dispatching of a series of event instances. During this traversal, the state machine executes a series of actions associated with various elements of the state machine."

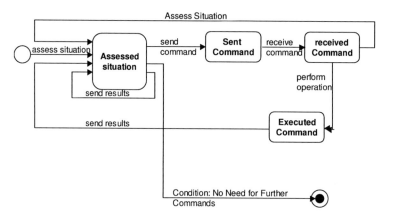

Figure 7.13 OV-6b Operational State Transition Description

Operational Event-Trace Description (OV-6c)

Product Purpose. "OV-6c is valuable for moving to the next level of detail from the initial operational concepts. The product helps define node interactions and operational threads. The OV-6c can also help ensure that each participating operational node has the necessary information it needs at the right time in order to perform its assigned operational activity."

Product Definition. "The Operational Event-Trace Description provides a time-ordered examination of the information exchanges between participating operational nodes as a result of a particular scenario. Each event-trace diagram should have an accompanying description that defines the particular scenario or situation."

Product Detailed Description. "OV-6c allows the tracing of actions in a scenario or critical sequence of events. OV-6c can be used by itself or in conjunction with OV-6b to describe the dynamic behavior of business processes or a mission/operational thread. An operational thread is defined as a set of operational activities, with sequence and timing attributes of the activities, and includes the information needed to accomplish the activities. A particular operational thread may be used to depict a capability. In this manner, a capability is defined in terms of the attributes required to accomplish a given mission objective by modeling the set of activities and their attributes."

The DoDAF suggests that architectures be executable. Actionable is a better word for today. To move in the executable direction, simulation must be used. In other words, the models must be made dynamic. The OV-6s are a step in that direction, but they remain static point in time models. The DoDAF suggests that IDEF3 is a choice for OV-6B and C. However, IDEF3 is not covered by a FIPS and is not recommended for this purpose.

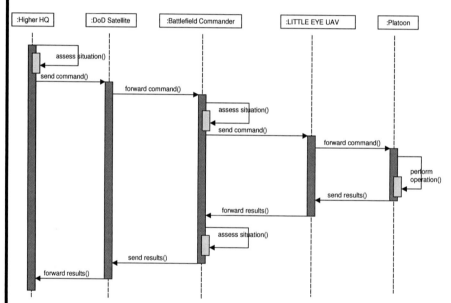

Figure 7.14 OV-6C Event Trace Description.

Logical Data Model (OV-7)

Product Purpose. "OV-7 including the domain's system data types or entity definitions is a key element in supporting interoperability between architectures, since these definitions may be used by other organizations to determine system data compatibility. Often, different organizations may use the same entity name to mean very different kinds of system data with different internal structure. This situation will pose significant interoperability risks, as the system data models may appear to be compatible, each having a *Target Track* data entity but having different and incompatible interpretations of what *Target Track* means."

"An OV-7 may be necessary for interoperability when shared system data syntax and semantics form the basis for greater degrees of information systems interoperability, or when a shared database is the basis for integration and interoperability among business processes and, at a lower level, among systems."

Product Definition. "The Logical Data Model describes the structure of an architecture domain's system data types and the structural business process rules (defined in the architecture's Operational View) that govern the system data. It provides a definition of architecture domain data types, their attributes or characteristics, and their interrelationships."

Product Detailed Description. "OV-7 defines the architecture domain's system data types (or entities) and the relationships among the system data types. For example, if the domain is missile defense, some possible system data types may be *trajectory* and *target* with a relationship that associates a target with a certain trajectory. On the other hand, architecture data types for the DoDAF (i.e., DoDAF-defined architecture data elements, AV-2 data types, and CADM entities) are things like an *operational node* or *operational activity*. OV-7 defines each kind of system data type associated with the architecture domain, mission, or business as its own entity, with its associated attributes and relationships. These entity definitions correlate to OV-3 information elements and OV-5 inputs, outputs, and controls."

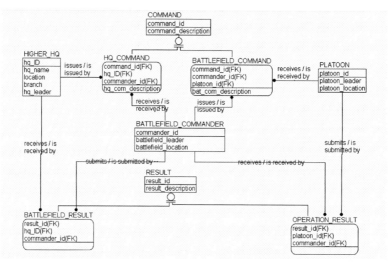

Figure 7.15 OV-7 Logical Data Model

OV-7 like OV-5 is governed by FIPS and there have existed multiple tools from various vendors that produce OV-7 IDEF1X Models. These models are interchangeable from one to another through the IDL.

The DoDAF suggests that specialization of UML Class Diagrams could also serve this purpose. While this is true, Why invent a methodology to do this when one exists?

This concludes our discussion of the OV products. Remember that the DoDAF suggests methods for producing products, it does not dictate them. The best product is the one that enables understanding of AS-IS and TO-BE operation that can lead to business process improvements and implementation of systems. Let's move on the Systems Views.

DoDAF says "The Systems View (SV) is a set of graphical and textual products that describe systems and interconnections providing for, or supporting, DoD functions. SV products focus on specific physical systems with specific physical (geographical) locations." Eleven SV Products are defined.

Systems Interface Description (SV-1)

Product Purpose. "SV-1 identifies systems nodes and systems that support operational nodes. Interfaces that cross organizational boundaries (key interfaces) can also be identified in this product. Some systems can have numerous interfaces. Initial versions of this product may only show key interfaces. Detailed versions may also be developed, as needed, for use in system acquisition, as part of requirements specifications, and for determining system interoperabilities at a finer level of technical detail."

Product Definition. "The Systems Interface Description depicts system's nodes and the systems resident at these nodes to support organizations/human roles represented by operational nodes of the Operational Node Connectivity Description (OV-2). SV-1 also identifies the interfaces between systems and systems nodes."

Product Detailed Description. "SV-1 links together the OV and SV by depicting the assignments of systems and systems nodes (and their associated interfaces) to the operational nodes (and their associated needlines) described in OV-2. OV-2 depicts the operational nodes representing organizations, organization types, and/or human roles, while SV-1 depicts the systems nodes that house operational nodes (e.g., platforms, units, facilities, and locations) and the corresponding systems resident at these systems nodes and which support the operational nodes. The term *system* in the framework is used to denote a family of systems (FoS), system of systems (SoS), nomenclatured system, or a subsystem. An item denotes a hardware or software item. Only systems, subsystems, or hardware/software items and their associated standards are documented in this product, where applicable. Details of the communications infrastructure (e.g., physical links, communications networks, routers, switches, communications systems, satellites) are documented in the Systems Communication Description (SV-2). In addition to depicting systems nodes and systems, SV-1 addresses system interfaces."

The DoDAF suggests UML Deployment Diagrams for SV-1 with embedded components. In UML, it has been seen that software components are considered to be the same as hardware components.

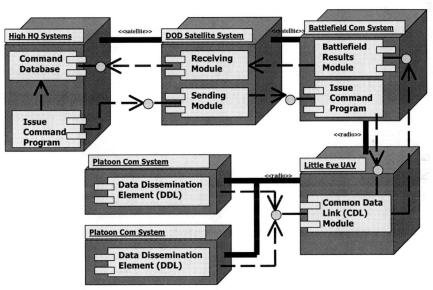

Figure 7.16 SV-1 Systems Interface Description

Systems Communications Description (SV-2)

Product Purpose. "SV-2 can be used to document how interfaces (described in SV-1) are supported by physical media. This kind of communications media support information is critical in performing certain infrastructure and system acquisition decisions."

Product Definition. "The Systems Communications Description depicts pertinent information about communications systems, communications links, and communications networks. SV-2 documents the kinds of communications media that support the systems and implement their interfaces as described in SV-1. Thus, SV-2 shows the communications details of SV-1 interfaces that automate aspects of the needlines represented in OV-2."

Product Detailed Description. "SV-2 documents the specific communications links or communications networks (e.g., Intelink or Joint Worldwide Intelligence Communications System [JWICS]) and the details of their configurations through which systems interface. While SV-1 depicts interfaces between systems or systems nodes, SV-2 contains a detailed description of how each SV-1 interface is implemented (e.g., composing parts of the implemented interface including communications systems, multiple communications links, communications networks."

The SV-2 should be the systems analog of the OV-2 and is better being a table than a diagram. But, the DoDAF says that it could be a UML Deployment Diagram. If so, there would need to be many, many notes.

Need line	Info Ex ID	Sending OP Node	Communications, Links, and Networks	Receiving OP Node
HQ Commands	1	Higher HQ (Command Server)	JWICS –IVp6	DoD Satellite (XP45 Router)
HQ Commands Via Satellite	2	DoD Satellite (XP45 Router)	JWICS–IVp6	Battlefield Commander (Com Server)
Battlefield Commands	3	Battlefield Commander (Com Server)	Intelink–IVp6	Little Eye (LE Router 3)
Battlefield Commands via Little Eye UAV	4	Little Eye (LE Router 3)	Intelink–IVp6	Platoon (Com Handset)
Operation Results	5	Platoon (Com Handset)	Intelink–IVp6	Little Eye (LE Router 3)
Operation Results Via Little Eye UAV	6	Little Eye (LE Router 3)	Intelink–IVp6	Battlefield Commander (Com Server)
Battlefield Operation Results	7	Battlefield Commander (Com Server)	JWICS–IVp6	DoD Satellite (XP45 Router)
Battlefield Operation Results Via Satellite	8	DoD Satellite (XP45 Router)	JWICS–IVp6	Higher HQ (Command Server)

Figure 7.17 SV-2 Systems Communications Description

Systems-Systems Matrix (SV-3)

Product Purpose. "SV-3 allows a quick overview of all the interface characteristics presented in multiple SV-1 diagrams. The matrix form can support a rapid assessment of potential commonalities and redundancies (or, if fault-tolerance is desired, the lack of redundancies). SV-3 can be organized in a number of ways (e.g., by domain, by operational mission phase) to emphasize the association of groups of system pairs in context with the architecture purpose. SV-3 can be a useful tool for managing the evolution of systems and system infrastructures, the insertion of new technologies/functionality, and the redistribution of systems and processes in context with evolving operational requirements."

Product Definition. "The Systems-Systems Matrix provides detail on the interface characteristics described in SV-1 for the architecture, arranged in matrix form."

Product Detailed Description. "SV-3 is a summary description of the system-system interfaces identified in SV-1. SV-3 is similar to an N^2-type matrix, where the systems are listed in the rows and columns of the matrix, and each cell indicates a system pair interface, if one exists. Many types of interface information can be presented in the cells of SV-3. The system-system interfaces can be represented using a number of different symbols and/or color codes that depict different interface characteristics."

SV-3 is analyzed by inspection. It is intended as a "quick look" at which systems talk to which systems. Of course, there is no UML representation of SV-3 or any other product that is text, table or matrix. Row and column headings trace to the systems of SV-1 and SV-2.

	LittleEye UAV	Higher HQ	DoD Sat	Battlefield Com	Platoon1 Com	Platoon2 Com
LittleEye UAV				●	●	●
Higher HQ			●			
DoD Sat		●		●		
Battlefield Com	●		●			
Platoon1 Com	●					
Platoon2 Com	●					

Figure 7.18 SV-3 Systems to Systems Matrix

Systems Functionality Description (SV-4)

Product Purpose. "The primary purposes of SV-4 are to (a) develop a clear description of the necessary system data flows that are input (consumed) by and output (produced) by each system, (b) ensure that the functional connectivity is complete (i.e., that a system's required inputs are all satisfied), and (c) ensure that the functional decomposition reaches an appropriate level of detail."

Product Definition. "The Systems Functionality Description documents system functional hierarchies and system functions, and the system data flows between them. Although there is a correlation between Operational Activity Model (OV-5) or business-process hierarchies and the system functional hierarchy of SV-4, it need not be a one-to-one mapping, hence, the need for the Operational Activity to Systems Function Traceability Matrix (SV-5), which provides that mapping."

Product Detailed Description. "SV-4 describes system functions and the flow of system data among system functions. It is the SV counterpart to OV-5." "The system functions documented in the SV-4 may be identified using the Service Component Reference Model (SRM)."

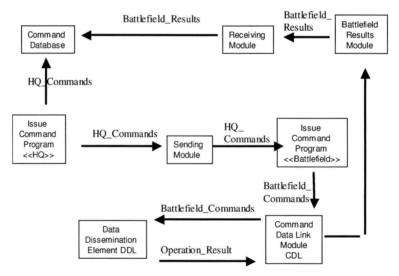

Figure 7.19 SV-4 Systems Functionality Description

Operational Activity to Systems Function Traceability Matrix (SV-5)

Product Purpose. "SV-5 depicts the mapping of operational activities to system functions and thus identifies the transformation of an operational need into a purposeful action performed by a system. SV-5 can be extended to depict the mapping of capabilities to operational activities, operational activities to system functions, system functions to systems, and thus relates the capabilities to the systems that support them. Such a matrix allows decision makers and planners to quickly identify stove piped systems, redundant/duplicative systems, gaps in capability, and possible future investment strategies all in accordance with the time stamp given to the architecture. SV-5 correlates capability requirements that would *not* be satisfied if a specific system is *not* fielded to a specific DoD unit."

Product Definition. "Operational Activity to Systems Function Traceability Matrix is a specification of the relationships between the set of operational activities applicable to an architecture and the set of system functions applicable to that architecture."

Product Detailed Description. "The Framework uses the terms *activity* in the OVs and *function* in the SVs to refer to essentially the same kind of thing—both activities and functions are tasks that are performed, accept inputs, and develop outputs. The distinction lies in the fact that system functions are executed by automated systems, while operational activities describe business operations that may be conducted by humans, automated systems, or both. Typical systems engineering practices use both of these terms, often interchangeably. However, given the Framework's use of activities on the operational side and functions on the systems side, and the fact that operational nodes do not map one-to-one to systems nodes, it is natural that operational activities do not map one-to-one to system functions. Therefore, SV-5 forms an integral part of the eventual complete mapping from operational capabilities to systems requirements. SV-5 is an explicit link between the OV and SV. The capabilities and activities are drawn from OV-5, OV-6b, and OV-6c. The system functions are drawn from an SV-4. SV-1 and SV-2 may also define system functions for identified systems."

SV-5 is an exact mapping between the Activities of the OV-5 and the system functions on the initial SVs. Depending on how the OV-5 mechanisms are defined, and the level of detail of the OV-5, this information may be exactly detailed in the IDEF0 mechanisms.

SYSTEMS SV-1/2	PROGRAM MODULES	Assess Situation	Send Commands	Receive Commands	Perform Operation	Send Results
High HQ Systems	Command Database	●	●			●
	Issue Command Program	●	●			
DoD Satellite Systems	Receiving Module					●
	Sending Module		●	●		
Battlefield COM System	Battlefield Results Module	●				●
	Issue Command Program		●	●		●
Little Eye UAV	Common Data Link Module (CDL)		●	●	●	●
Platoon Com System	Data Dissemination Element (DDE)			●	●	●

Figure 7.20 SV-5 Operational Activity to Systems Function Traceability Matrix

Systems Data Exchange Matrix (SV-6)

Product Purpose. "System data exchanges express the relationship across the three basic architecture data elements of an SV (systems, system functions, and system data flows) and focus on the specific aspects of the system data flow and the system data content. These aspects of the system data exchange can be crucial to the operational mission and are critical to understanding the potential for overhead and constraints introduced by the physical aspects of the implementation."

Product Definition. "The Systems Data Exchange Matrix specifies the characteristics of the system data exchanged between systems. This product focuses on automated information exchanges (from OV-3) that are implemented in systems. Non-automated information exchanges, such as verbal orders, are captured in the OV products only."

Product Detailed Description. "SV-6 describes, in tabular format, system data exchanged between systems. The focus of SV-6 is on how the system data exchange is implemented, in system-specific details covering periodicity, timeliness, throughput, size, information assurance, and security characteristics of the exchange. In addition, the system data elements, their format and media type, accuracy, units of measurement, and system data standard are also described in the matrix. SV-6 relates to, and grows out of, OV-3. The operational characteristics for the OV-3 information exchange are replaced with the corresponding system data characteristics. For example, the Levels of Information Systems Interoperability (LISI) level required for the operational information exchange is replaced by the LISI level achieved through the system data exchange(s). Similarly, performance attributes for the operational information exchanges are replaced by the actual system data exchange performance attributes for the automated portion(s) of the information exchange. On SV-6, each operational needline is decomposed into the interfaces that are the systems."

IER #	Sender	Receiver	Content	Media	Format	Freq.	Time	Throughput
1	Issue Command Program (HQ)	Sending Module	Command	SAT-Trans	SATMAT	N/A	5sec	1GB/sec
2	Issue Command Program (HQ)	Command Database	Sent Command	N/A	SQL	N/A	5sec	100MB/sec
3	Sending Module	Issue Command Program (Battlefield)	Forwarded Command	SAT-Trans	SATMAT	N/A	5sec	1GB/sec
4	Issue Command Program (Battlefield)	Command Data Link Module (CDL)	Battlefield Command	CDL-UAV	Voice, data,	N/A	N/A	100mb/sec
5	Command Data Link Module (CDL)	Data Dissemination Element (DDE)	Battlefield Command	DDE	Voice, data,	N/A	N/A	100mb/sec
6	Data Dissemination Element (DDE)	Command Data Link Module (CDL)	Operation Result	DDE	Voice, data,	N/A	10sec	100mb/sec

Figure 7.21 SV-6 Systems Data Exchange Matrix

Systems Performance Parameters Matrix (SV-7)

Product Purpose. "One of the primary purposes of SV-7 is to communicate which characteristics are considered most crucial for the successful achievement of the mission goals assigned to the system. These particular parameters can often be the deciding factors in acquisition and deployment decisions, and will figure strongly in systems analyses and simulations done to support the acquisition decision processes and system design refinement."

Product Definition. "The Systems Performance Parameters Matrix product specifies the quantitative characteristics of systems and system hardware/software items, their interfaces (system data carried by the interface as well as communications link details that implement the interface), and their functions. It specifies the current performance parameters of each system, interface, or system function, and the expected or required performance parameters at specified times in the future. Performance parameters include all technical performance characteristics of systems for which requirements can be developed and specification defined. The complete set of performance parameters may not be known at the early stages of architecture definition, so it should be expected that this product will be updated throughout the system's specification, design, development, testing, and possibly even its deployment and operations life-cycle phases."

Product Detailed Description. "SV-7 builds on SV-1, SV-2, SV-4, and SV-6 by specifying performance parameters for systems and system hardware/software items and their interfaces (defined in SV-1), communications details (defined in SV-2), their functions (defined in SV-4), and their system data exchanges (defined in SV-6). The term *system*, as defined for this product and all others in the Framework, may represent a family of systems (FoS), system of systems (SoS), network of systems, or an individual system. Performance parameters for system hardware/software items (the hardware and software elements comprising a system) are also described in this product. In addition, performance parameters often relate to a system function being performed. Therefore, system functions and their performance attributes may also be shown in this product. If the future performance expectations are based on expected technology improvements, then the performance parameters and their time periods should be coordinated with a Systems Technology Forecast (SV-9). If performance improvements are associated with an overall system evolution or migration plan, then the time periods in SV-7 should be coordinated with the milestones in an Systems Evolution Description (SV-8)."

DoDAF provides a "template" table that can have many interpretations for SV-7. The key is to keep in mind that SV-7 is expected to be system's performance in support of the business performance.

System Name	Performance Range Thresholds and Measures			
	Internet Protocol	Processor Speed	RAM	......
High HQ System	IPv6	3.60GHz	512MB	...
DoD Satellite System	IPv6	2.5GHz	1,064 MBps (DDR SDRAM)	...
Battlefield COM System	IPv6	2.2GHz	256MB	...
Little Eye UAV	IPv6	733MHz	256MB	...
Platoon COM	IPv6	733MHz	128MB	...

Figure 7.22 SV-7 Systems Performance Parameters Matrix

Systems Evolution Description (SV-8)

Product Purpose. "SV-8, when linked together with other evolution products such as SV-9 and TV-2, provides a clear definition of how the architecture and its systems are expected to evolve over time. In this manner, the product can be used as an architecture evolution project plan or transition plan."

Product Definition. "The Systems Evolution Description captures evolution plans that describe how the system, or the architecture in which the system is embedded, will evolve over a lengthy period of time. Generally, the timeline milestones are critical for a successful understanding of the evolution timeline."

Product Detailed Description. "SV-8 describes plans for *modernizing* system functions over time. Such efforts typically involve the characteristics of *evolution* (spreading in scope while increasing functionality and flexibility) or *migration* (incrementally creating a more streamlined, efficient, smaller, and cheaper suite) and will often combine the two thrusts. This product builds on other products and analyses in that planned capabilities and information requirements that relate to performance parameters (of SV-7) and technology forecasts (of SV-9) are accommodated in this product."

Think the inverse of root cause analysis i.e., the classic fishbone chart for this product.

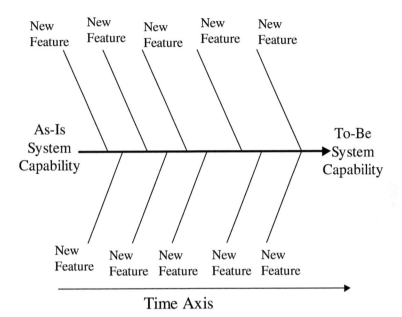

Figure 7.23 SV-8 Systems Evolution Description

Here, the architect looks at the TO-BE and works backwards to the present in terms of what is necessary to deliver new features and new capabilities over the system life cycle.

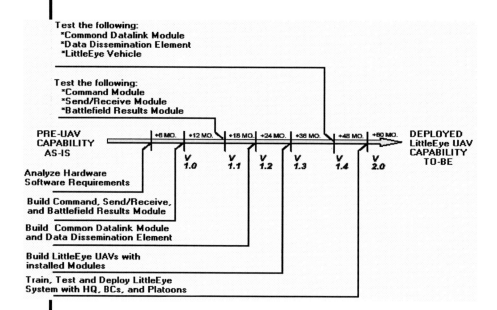

Figure 7.24 SV-8 for our common example

Systems Technology Forecast (SV-9)

Product Purpose. "SV-9 provides a summary of emerging technologies that impact the architecture and its existing planned systems. The focus should be on the supporting technologies that may most affect the capabilities of the architecture or its systems."

Product Definition. "The Systems Technology Forecast defines the underlying current and expected supporting technologies. It is not expected to include predictions of technologies as with a crystal ball. Expected supporting technologies are those that can be reasonably forecast given the current state of technology and expected improvements. New technologies should be tied to specific time periods, which can correlate against the time periods used in SV-8 milestones."

Product Detailed Description. "SV-9 provides a detailed description of emerging technologies and specific hardware and software products. It contains predictions about the availability of emerging technological capabilities and about industry trends in specific time periods. The specific time periods selected (e.g., 6-month, 12-month, 18-month intervals) and the technologies being tracked should be coordinated with architecture transition plans (see SV-8). That is, insertion of new technological capabilities and upgrading of existing systems may depend on or be driven by the availability of new technology. The forecast includes potential technology impacts on current architectures and thus influences the development of transition and objective (i.e., target) architectures. The forecast should be focused on technology areas that are related to the purpose for which a given architecture is being described and should identify issues that will affect the architecture. If standards are an integral part of the technologies important to the evolution of a given architecture, then it may be convenient to combine SV-9 with the Technical Standards Forecast (TV-2). SV-9 is constructed as part of a given architecture"

JTA Service	TECHNOLOGY FORECAST		
	0-6 Mo	6-18 Mo	Long Term
APPLICATION SOFTWARE			
Support Applications	Requirements Analysis for: •Receiving Module •Sending Module •Command Program •Battlefield Results Module •Common Data Link •Data Dissemination Element	Develop build for: •Receiving Module •Sending Module •Command Program •Battlefield Results Module •Common Data Link •Data Dissemination Element	Upgrades to modules, command programs, data links and element support applications are continual.
APPLICATION ENVIRONMENT			
Data Management	Requirements Analysis for: Command Database	Develop build for: Command Database	Future integration with DoD National Command Database (DODNCD)
Operating System	MS Windows Server MS Windows Client WAP OS	MS Windows Server MS Windows Client WAP OS	Future Integrated DoD OS System (DODOS)
Physical Environment	DoD Satellite / LittleEye UAV	DoD Satellite / LittleEye UAV /Platoon Handheld Com	Future upgrades to DoD Satellite and LittleEye UAVs
EXTERNAL ENVIRONMENT			
User Interface	Field – Handheld PDA	Field – Handheld PDA	Field – Handheld PDA
Persistent Storage	Data Dissemination Element includes 5G PCMCIA Card.	Data Dissemination Element will includes 16G PCMCIA Card.	Disk Storage doubles again
Communications Networks	GIG, JTRS, WINTS	GIG, JTRS, WINTS	GIG, JTRS, WINTS

Figure 7.25 SV-9 Systems Technology Forecast

As the three OV-6 products described the business rules and the dynamic characteristics of operations activities, there are three SVs that perform the same purpose for the Systems Views. These are the SV-10 products for Systems Functionality Sequence and Timing Descriptions. There are three SV10's:

Systems Rules Model (SV-10a)
Systems State Transition Description (SV-10b)
Systems Event-Trace Description (SV-10c)

"Systems Rules Model (SV-10a)

Product Purpose. "The purpose of this product is to allow understanding of behavioral rules and constraints imposed on systems and system functions."

Product Definition. "Systems rules are constraints on an architecture, on a system(s), or system hardware/software item(s), and/or on a system function(s). While other SV products (e.g., SV-1, SV-2, SV-4, SV-11) describe the static structure of the Systems View (i.e., what the systems can do), they do not describe, for the most part, what the systems *must* do, or what it *cannot* do. At the systems or system hardware/software items level, SV-10a describes the rules under which the architecture or its systems behave under specified conditions. At lower levels of decomposition, it may consist of rules that specify the pre- and post-conditions of system functions. Such rules can be expressed in a textual form, for example, "If (these conditions) exist, and (this event) occurs, then (perform these actions)."

Product Detailed Description. *"Rules are statements that define or constrain some aspect of the enterprise.* In contrast to the Operational Rules Model (OV-6a), SV-10a focuses on constraints imposed by some aspect of operational performance requirements that translate into system performance requirements. At a lower level of detail, it focuses on some aspects of systems design or implementation. Thus, as the operational rules can be associated with the Operational Activity Model (OV-5), the systems rules in SV-10a can be associated with SV-1 and SV-2 systems and hardware/software items or with SV-4 system functions."

SYSTEM RULES MODEL:

Receiving Module Rules:
If Operation Results are received *then* forward Operation Results to Command Database, *else* remain idle.
If Operation Results transmission *is* incomplete *then* send error message "Incomplete Transmission" to Battlefield Results Module.

Data Dissemination Element Rules:
For every Battlefield Command received do:
  1) Prioritize Command
  2) Display "New Command Received" to Platoon Leader
  3) Place Command in Queue
When Battlefield Command *is* completed *then* send Operation Results.

Figure 7.26 Systems Rules Model (SV-10a)

Systems State Transition Description (SV-10b)

Product Purpose. "The explicit time sequencing of system functions in response to external and internal events is not fully expressed in SV-4. SV-10b can be used to describe the explicit sequencing of the system functions. Alternatively, SV-10b can be used to reflect explicit sequencing of the actions internal to a single system function, or the sequencing of system functions with respect to a specific system. Basically, statechart diagrams can be unambiguously converted to structured textual rules that specify timing aspects of systems events and the responses to these events, with no loss of meaning. However, the graphical form of the state diagrams can often allow quick analysis of the completeness of the rule set, and detection of dead ends or missing conditions. These errors, if not detected early during the systems analysis phase, can often lead to serious behavioral errors in fielded systems, or to expensive correction efforts."

Product Definition. "The Systems State Transition Description is a graphical method of describing a system (or system function) response to various events by changing its state. The diagram basically represents the sets of events to which the systems in the architecture will respond (by taking an action to move to a new state) as a function of its current state. Each transition specifies an event and an action."

Product Detailed Description. "SV-10b is based on the state chart diagram [OMG, 2003]. A state machine is defined as "a specification that describes all possible behaviors of some dynamic model element. Behavior is modeled as a traversal of a graph of state nodes interconnected by one or more joined transition arcs that are triggered by the dispatching of series of event instances. During this traversal, the state machine executes a series of actions associated with various elements of the state machine." "SV-10b can be used to describe the detailed sequencing of system functions described in SV-4"

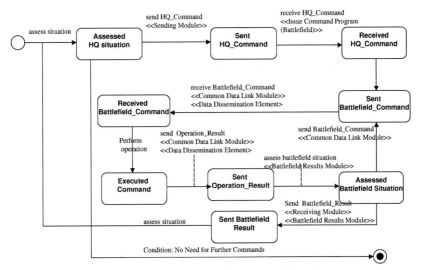

Figure 7.27 Systems State Diagram (SV-10b)

Systems Event-Trace Description (SV-10c)

Product Purpose. "SV-10c products are valuable for moving to the next level of detail from the initial systems design, to help define a sequence of functions and system data interfaces, and to ensure that each participating system, system function, or human role has the necessary information it needs, at the right time, in order to perform its assigned functionality."

Product Definition. "The Systems Event-Trace Description provides a time-ordered examination of the system data elements exchanged between participating systems (external and internal), system functions, or human roles as a result of a particular scenario. Each event-trace diagram should have an accompanying description that defines the particular scenario or situation. SV-10c in the Systems View may reflect system-specific aspects or refinements of critical sequences of events described in the Operational View."

Product Detailed Description. "SV-10c allows the tracing of actions in a scenario or critical sequence of events. With time proceeding from the top of the diagram to the bottom, a specific diagram lays out the sequence of system data exchanges that occur between system (external and internal), system functions, or human role for a given scenario. Different scenarios should be depicted by separate diagrams. SV-10c can be used by itself or in conjunction with a SV-10b to describe dynamic behavior of system"

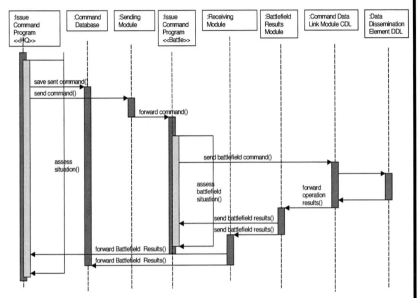

Figure 7.28 Systems Event Trace Description SV-10c

5.11.1 Physical Schema (SV-11)

Product Purpose. "The product serves several purposes, including (a) providing as much detail as possible on the system data elements exchanged between systems, thus reducing the risk of interoperability errors, and (b) providing system data structures for use in the system design process, if necessary."

Product Definition. "The Physical Schema product is one of the architecture products closest to actual system design in the Framework. The product defines the structure of the various kinds of system data that are utilized by the systems in the architecture."

Product Detailed Description. "SV-11 is an implementation-oriented data model that is used in the Systems View to describe how the information requirements represented in Logical Data Model (OV-7) are actually implemented. Entities represent (a) system data flows in SV-4, (b) system data."

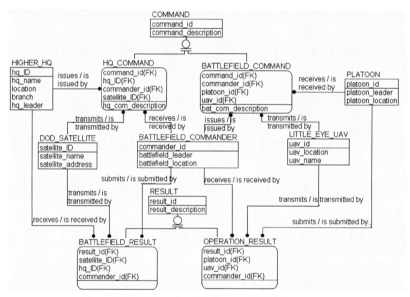

Figure 7.29 Physical Schema SV-11

Technical Standards Profile (TV-1)

"Product Purpose. Primarily, this product is concerned with delineating systems standards rules and conventions that apply to architecture implementations. When the standards profile is tied to the system elements to which they apply, TV-1 serves as the bridge between the SV and TV."

Product Definition. The Technical Standards Profile collects the various systems standards rules that implement and sometimes constrain the choices that can be made in the design and implementation of an architecture."

Product Detailed Description. "TV-1 consists of the set of systems standards rules that govern systems implementation and operation of that architecture. The technical standards generally govern what hardware and software may be implemented and what system data formats may be used (i.e., the profile delineates which standards may be used to implement the systems, system hardware/software items, communications protocols, and system data formats). TV-1 is constructed as part of a given architecture and in accordance with the architecture purpose."

The TV-1 example describes each standard that is applicable to each system as it relates to each service standards that are currently applicable to each JTA service in the enterprise architecture. Documenting and understanding the standards is a tedious yet important process to building the EA.

Advice here is to begin with the Joint Technical Architecture – the JTA.

The JTA is the basis for the Technical Standards Profile. Again, the specific process depends on the specific customer.

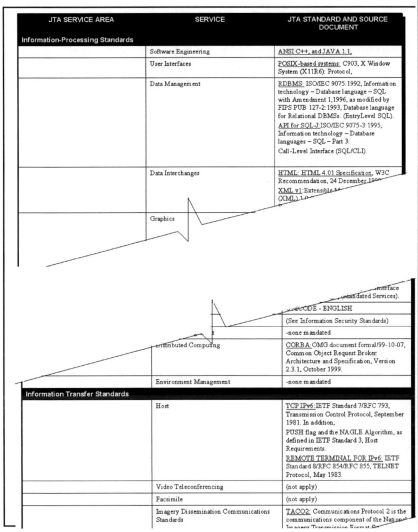

Figure 7.30 Technical Standards Profile TV-1

Technical Standards Forecast (TV-2)

Product Purpose. "One of the prime purposes of this product is to identify critical technology standards, their fragility, and the impact of these standards on the future development and maintainability of the architecture and its constituent elements."

Product Definition. "The Technical Standards Forecast contains expected changes in technology-related standards and conventions, which are documented in the TV-1 product. The forecast for evolutionary changes in the standards should be correlated against the time periods as mentioned in the SV-8 and SV-9 products."

Product Detailed Description. "TV-2 lists emerging or evolving technology standards relevant to the systems covered by the architecture. It contains predictions about the availability of emerging standards, and relates these predictions to the Systems View elements and the time periods that are listed in the SV-8 and SV-9. The specific time periods selected (e.g., 6-month, 12-month, 18-month intervals) depend on the nature of the EA."

| TECHNOLOGY STANDARDS FORECAST ||||
| JTA Service: Software Engineering ||||
SYSTEMS:	0-6 Mo	6-18 Mo	Long Term
High HQ Systems	ANSI C++, and JAVA 1.1	ANSI C++, and JAVA 1.1	C++ code base migration to C# language, and JAVA 1.1 code migration to JAVA 2.0 compatibility
DoD Satellite System	ANSI C++,	ANSI C++,	C++ code base recompiled into C# language,
Battlefield Com System	ANSI C++,	ANSI C++,	C++ code base recompiled into C# language,
LittleEye UAV System	ANSI C++,	ANSI C++,	C++ code base recompiled into C# language,
Platoon Com System	JAVA 1.1	JAVA 1.1	JAVA 1.1 code migration to JAVA 2.0 compatibility

| TECHNOLOGY STANDARDS FORECAST ||||
| JTA Service: Data Interchanges ||||
SYSTEMS:	0-6 Mo	6-18 Mo	Long Term
High HQ Systems	HTML: HTML 4.01 Specification, W3C Recommendation, 24 December 1999. XML v1:Extensible Markup Language (XML) 1.0 (Second Edition), W3C Recommendation,6 October 2000.	HTML: HTML 4.01 Specification, W3C Recommendation, 24 December 1999. XML v1:Extensible Markup Language (XML) 1.0 (Second Edition), W3C Recommendation,6 October 2000.	Move to HTML 6.0 and XML v2
DoD Satellite System			
Battlefield Com System	ANSI C++, HTML: HTML 4.01 Specification, W3C Recommendation, 24 December 1999. XML v1:Extensible Markup Language (XML) 1.0 (Second Edition), W3C Recommendation,6 October 2000.	HTML: HTML 4.01 Specification, W3C Recommendation, 24 December 1999. XML v1:Extensible Markup Language (XML) 1.0 (Second Edition), W3C Recommendation,6 October 2000.	Move to HTML 6.0 and XML v2
LittleEye UAV System			
Platoon Com System	HTML: HTML 4.01 Specification, W3C Recommendation, 24 December 1999. XML v1:Extensible Markup Language (XML) 1.0 (Second Edition), W3C Recommendation,6 October 2000.	HTML: HTML 4.01 Specification, W3C Recommendation, 24 December 1999. XML v1:Extensible Markup Language (XML) 1.0 (Second Edition), W3C Recommendation,6 October 2000.	Move to HTML 6.0 and XML v2

Figure 7.31 TV-2 Technical Standards Forecast Example

OK, do I really need to know about 26 products?

This chapter provided a purpose, definition, description, and an example for every product of the 26 products that are used to describe a DoDAF.

Also in this chapter, it was demonstrated how IDEF0, IDEF1X, and the various diagramming constructs of UML have contributed to an affective description of the DoDAF. Understand that each work product describes but one essential dimension of the overall DoDAF. Also understand that as the requirements for DoDAF evolve, new work products will be identified, and existing ones refined for an even a more accurate description of the DoDAF. As a DoDAF architect, you the reader must keep a finger on the pulse of these DoDAF requirements.

While this chapter described the "What." The next chapter presents the *Minimalist Methodology*- "How" applied to an example with the 15 minimal products for DoDAF essential, 6212.01c and NCOW.

Chapter Eight

Let's Build an Enterprise Architecture

Coming together is a beginning, staying together is progress, and working together is success.
- HENRY FORD

The Scenario (fictitious)

The face of war is changing. The traditional battlefield with clear front lines and clear distinctions between friend and foe is giving way to urbanized warfare. Urbanized warfare presents many more dangers than other wartime activities. The current military experience has brought home many lessons learned, and revealed a deep need for safer alternatives that can spare the lives of those soldiers fighting in urban campaigns.

A diverse group of military veterans came together to form MANDROID INC. They established the following mission:

"To provide safer alternatives, that can spare the lives of those soldiers fighting in campaigns abroad."

The founders of MANDROID INC. seek to utilize current technology trends in robotics, energy, sensors and manufacturing to create products that will provide DoD with a 'safer alternative' than front line humans fighting in urban environments.

MANDROID INC.'s response to a 'safer alternative' was the MANDROID product line. The MANDROID seems autonomous in its movement and interaction with the environment. Riding on a wheeled base, it has arms, a torso, a head, and moves fluidly much like a human. The MANDROID speaks audibly, sometimes with an accent. It also listens, and replies when spoken to. One would think it to be self-aware and intelligent; however, a human operator several miles away operates MANDROID by remote control. This product was not designed to replace the soldier, but to keep the soldier farther from harm's way.

Figure 8.1 MANDROIDS on Patrol

MANDROID control centers contain the human operators a.k.a. MANDROID specialists who actually control the MANDROID.

Before a broad DoD audience, MANDROID INC. demonstrated its first Hydrogen fuel cell powered MANDROID prototype. The results were impressive, and the response was overwhelming. MANDROID INC., determined that MANDROIDS could be made inexpensively, costing the equivalent to the first year salary of a newly enlisted soldier. MANDROID INC. was ready to do major business with the DoD, and the DoD was ready to place an order for a product that will save many lives on the battlefields of today and tomorrow. However, there was one problem: the MANDROID project was not compliant with the DoDAF. There was a need for a MANDROID architecture showing how MANDROID would comply with the DoD requirement to be "born joint."

MANDROID INC. employed the services of Wizdom System Inc. Wizdom's DoDAF software and consulting expertise will provide MANDROID INC. with the work products it needed to be DoDAF compliant.

The Minimalist Methodology Applied

MANDROID INC will follow Wizdom's 11-step methodology outlined in Chapter 3 to complete the minimal set of products required. Wizdom Systems Inc., along with MANDROID INC will proceed to build all of the DoDAF work products listed on the next page.

STEP #	STEP NAME / WORK PRODUCTS / DURATION
1	Develop Overview and Summary Info AV-1 AV-2
2	Build Operational Activity Models OV-1 OV-5
3	Build Org. Relationships Chart, Logical / Physical Data Model, and Systems Functionality Descriptions OV-4 OV-7 SV-4 SV-11
4	Build Operational Event Trace Description and System Event Trace Description OV-6C SV-10C
5	Build Operational Informational Exchange Matrix OV-3 OV-6A
6	Build Operational State Transition Description and Systems State Transition Description OV-6B SV-10B
7	Build Operations Node Connectivity Diagram OV-2
8	Build Systems Interface Description (Components) SV-1
9	Build Function, Tractability and Data Exchange Matrices SV-5 SV-6
10	Build Systems Interface Description (Deployment) SV-1
11	Build and Maintain the Technical Standards Profile TV-1

Figure 8.2 Wizdom Minimalist Methodology Timeline

As shown in the figure, there is overlap among the steps because work products are all interrelated. Many work products will be developed in parallel as team members collaborate to build them. Steps 1, 2 and 11 continue for the life of the project as they are revised and reworked.

Tools for Architecture
Architects of today and yesterday agree that great ideas and concepts require the use of good, reliable tools. As an

architect of a building uses rulers, scales, T-squares, drafting boards, mechanical pencils, and now Computer Aided Design (CAD) tools to build structures, Wizdom comes to MANDROID INC. with a tool chest of its own. At the start of the project, Wizdom meets with MANDROID project management to recommend a partial list of tools that will be used to build the DoDAF architecture.

Work Product	Tool(s) Recommended	Project Management Tool Recommended
AV-1	Process*Works*!, MS WORD	**DoDAF*Live!***
AV-2	Process*Works*!	
OV-1	Process*Works*!	**Features Include:**
OV-2	Process*Works*!	• **100% web based**
OV-3	**Bonapart!**	• **Manages the DoDAF work product life cycle.**
OV-4	Process*Works*!	
OV-5	Process*Works*!, MS VISIO	• **Built-in Gantt charts for work product development**
OV-6a	Data*Works!*	• **Templates for each work product**
OV-6b	**Bonapart!**	
OV-6c	**Bonapart!**	• **MS OUTLOOK Compatible**
OV-7	Data*Works!*	• **MS PROJECT Compatible**
SV-1	**Bonapart!**	• **WAP Compatible**
SV-4	Process*Works*!	• **Document Management**
SV-5	MS EXCEL	• **Calendaring and Resource Management**
SV-6	MS EXCEL	
SV-10b	**Bonapart!**	• **Collaboration and Instant Messaging**
SV-10c	**Bonapart!**	
SV-11	Data*Works!*	
TV-1	MS EXCEL	

Figure 8.3 DoDAF Tools Recommendations

When the project team project managers agree on the final list of tools from the previous table above, Steps 1, 2 and 11 of Wizdom's Minimalist Methodology begins. The importance of a DoDAF project management tool and its role in managing the overall DoDAF project initiative can not be overemphasized. DoDAF work products are living documents, and will evolve with the architecture that they describe. It is crucial to have an interactive tool to guide the project steps, communicate between team members and store documents and products in context as they are built.

The Wizdom project manager's first task is to start a brand new enterprise area in a project management tool - here **DoDAFLive!** This area will serve as the base from which teams will collaborate and build all future and evolving DoDAF work products. As a new enterprise area, it will provide valuable template and step-by-step information that will help minimize the development time needed to complete a DoDAF product.

The project manager's second task is to obtain team information about all those who will be participating in the MANDROID DoDAF project. This includes names, titles, addresses, phones, and email addresses. The project manager will enter these once into **DoDAFLive!** where teams will be formed and collaborate to build work products.

The Wizdom project manager's final task before starting the initiative is to train MANDROID INC. project managers and personnel. This training will include educating them on the significance of DoDAF Wizdom's 11-step Minimalist Methodology, and the important role that **DoDAF*Live!*** will play over the course of the initiative.

STEP 1: DEVELOP OVERVIEW and SUMMARY INFORMATION

DoDAF compliance begins with a series of facilitated meetings with the project team management to discuss and educate the MANDROID managers on the importance of DoDAF and the kinds of products that will be required to be DoDAF compliant. Through these sessions the Wizdom team will begin to paint a clear picture of the MANDROID INC. enterprise and its relationship with the DoD client. MANDROID INC. operations are extensive, and the DoD client has particular interest in the architecture that will provide Born Joint Combat Ready MANDROID Units to the front line.

Wizdom and MANDROID executives agree on the name and purpose of this project:

Project name: *BORN JOINT COMBAT READY SUPPORT PROJECT*

Purpose: *"To define an architecture that will provide MANDROID INC. with the capability to support the DoD with BORN JOINT COMBAT READY MANDROID UNITS."* Wizdom facilitators work with high-level MANDROID executives to further define an overview of this architecture project. This high-level overview -also known as the '*AV-1*

Overview and Summary Information' - becomes the first of many DoDAF work products.

Figure 8.4 AV-1

Architecture Project Identification	
• Name	JIT COMBAT READY MANDROID SUPPORT PROJECT
• Architect	WIZDOM SYSTEMS INC.
• Organization Developing the Architecture	MANDROID Inc.
• Assumptions and Constraints	**Constraint** Budget: $650,000 - with 1 year to complete.
• Approval Authority	OMB
• Date Completed	(in process)
Scope: Architecture View(s) and Products Identification	
• Views and Products Developed	(AV1), (AV2), (OV1), (OV2), (OV-3), (OV4), (OV5), (OV6a), (OV6b), (OV6c), (OV7), (SV1), (SV4), (SV5), (SV6), (SV10b), (SV10c), (SV11), (TV1)
• Time Frames Addressed	Jan 2 04 –Mar. 2 04: (AV1), (AV2), (OV1), (OV5), (OV4), Mar 2 04 – May 2 04: (OV3), (OV6c), (SV10c), (OV7), (SV4), (SV11), May 2 04 – Jul 2 04: (OV2), (SV10b), (OV6a), (OV6b) Jul 2 04 – Jan 2 05 (TV1), (SV1), (SV5), (SV6),
• Organizations Involved	MANDROID INC., WIZDOM SYSTEMS INC., DoD
Purpose and Viewpoint	
• Purpose, Analysis, Questions to be answered by Analysis of the Architecture	**Project Purpose:** To define an architecture that will provide MANDROID INC. with the capability to support the DoD with JIT COMBAT READY MANDROID UNITS. **Analysis:** Will review the views necessary to accomplish the project's purpose **Questions:** Does MANDROID INC. have the capability to provide JIT COMBAT READY MANDROID SUPPORT?
• From Whose Viewpoint the Architecture is Developed	Viewpoint is from Director of JIT MANDROID SUPPORT
Context	
• Mission	**Mission:** To provide JIT COMBAT READY MANDRIOD UNITS to the DoD as they are needed.
• Doctrine, Goals, and Vision	**Goals:** *To have a COMBAT READY MANDROID UNIT assembled, tested, and available for delivery within 24 Hours of DoD demand.
• Rules, Criteria, and Conventions Followed	**Rules:** *MANDROID UNITS will be manufactured and replaced by MANDROID INC. as sensory systems on active units have confirmed casualty/disability in the field of combat. **(N) number of MANDROID UNITS will be manufactured as demand is identified by the DoD
• Tasking for Architecture Project linkages to Other Architectures	**Tasks:** *Integrate with MANUFACTURING MRP ARCHITECTURES *Integrate with DoD ACQUISITIONS ARCHITECTURES
Tools and File Formats Used:	
	DoDAF*Live*!, Process*Works*!, Data*Works*!, MSWORD, MSPROJECT,
Findings	
• Analysis Results	<In Process>
• Recommendations	<In Process>

Consultants learn the terms that drive their client. As the AV-1 is completed, (AV-2) is revised. The greatest benefit to having this dictionary is the ability to quickly communicate to new partners, vendors, and customers.

> Printed 10/8/2004
> Glossary Report
> 6
> PROJECT: JIT COMBAT READY SUPPORT
>
> **MANAGE PRODUCTION ORDER (Activity)**
> This activity takes order requirements to generate a production order. This activity also monitors the progress of the production order all throughout the assembly and delivery phases of the MANDROID order.
> Used At:
>   A13:REVIEW DEMAND AND MANAGE PRODUCTION ORDER
>
> **MANAssembly Plant (Arrow)**
> The location at which MANDROIDS are assembled and await pickup for use by DoD.
> Used At:
>   A-0:MANAGE JIT COMBAT READY MANDROID SUPPORT[CONTEXT]
>
> **MANDROID (Arrow)**
> A human-like robotic device with human-like physical capabilities that operates in hostil environments where human life may be compromised. This device is remotely controlled in real time by MANDROID specialists who are located remotely at mobile and control centers world-wide.
> Used At:
>   A-0:MANAGE JIT COMBAT READY MANDROID SUPPORT[CONTEXT]
>
> **MANDROID Airstrip (Arrow)**
> The airstrip used by DoD to pickup Combat Ready MANDROIDS.
> Used At:
>   A0:MANAGE BORN JOINT COMBAT READY MANDROID SUPPORT
>   A4:SCHEDULE PICKUP
>
> **MANDROID Armaments (Arrow)**
> Weapon systems that are compatible with the MANDROID. Systems include: laser guided assult rifel, grenade launcher, gas cannon, infrared display, and a nuclear core with a low-yield detonation equivalent of up to .5 Kilotons.
> Used At:
>   A0:MANAGE BORN JOINT COMBAT READY MANDROID SUPPORT
>   A2:ASSEMBLE MANDROIDS

Figure 8.5 Partial AV-2

As work products evolve, the '*AV-2: Integrated Dictionary*' becomes a solid foundation for understanding and future expansion of the architecture. During the facilitations, Analysts capture terms and their meanings in a software tool integrated with DoDAF products. This tool is used by the project team throughout the project as the *AV-2* continues to grow and evolve with the architecture.

STEP 2: BUILD OPERATIONAL ACTIVITY MODELS

With the AV-1 and AV-2 work products underway; the project team begins to build a set of high-level graphics that describe the overall operations of MANDROID INC. DoDAF describes the OV-1 as a high level graphical depiction. Experience shows that this is not sufficient. The OV-1 should be matched to an IDEF A-0 and perhaps its equivalent Use-Case and text.

This description will provide the viewer with a high level understanding of MANDROID INC. as a whole. When DoDAF architects begin to review MANDROID INC.'s work products, they will need to know at a high-level where MANDROID INC. operations fit in with the rest of the framework.

This graphic will illustrate at a 10,000-foot level the scope of the BORN JOINT COMBAT SUPPORT PROJECT. With the help of graphic artists, the project team completes an *OV-1* that depicts MANDROID INC.'s supply of DoD's demand for MANDROID units in the battlefield.

From a completed *OV-1*, the team has a graphic that can be used to communicate the scope of the project and serve as basis for future discussions. It will be from this graphic that the project team will further define the architecture that *"...will provide MANDROID INC. with the capability to support the DoD with BORN JOINT COMBAT READY MANDROID UNITS."* That is, satisfy the purpose.

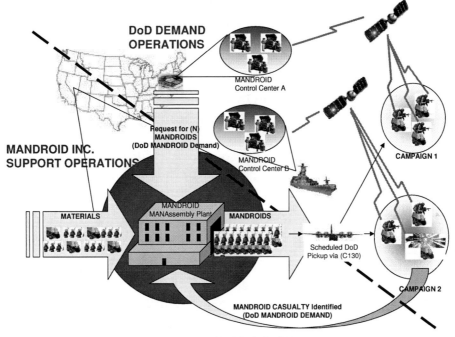

Figure 8.6 MANDROID OV-1

Experience shows that problems are better solved when broken down into manageable 'parts.' Wizdom applies this same understanding to the problem of understanding the details behind MANDROID INC.'s operational processes. Through a series of facilitated sessions with MANDROID INC executive teams and supporting staff, Wizdom will apply the government supported IDEF0 (FIPS pub 183) activity modeling methodology to define a structured, hierarchical view of the activities that drive MANDROID INC.

Wizdom breaks out the *OV-1* before the team and asks them to review the graphic for some of the various operational activities that are implied in the diagram. The facilitator wants them to keep in mind the purpose and viewpoint of the project as identified in the AV-1. The facilitator displays this on the board as a reminder to them:

Purpose: *"To define an architecture that will provide MANDROID INC. with the capability to support the DoD with BORN JOINT COMBAT READY MANDROID UNITS."*

Viewpoint: *Director of BORN JOINT MANDROID SUPPORT*

With purpose and viewpoint in mind, the team comes up with a list of activities. As members list off activities, the Wizdom facilitator places them on the board:
- Detect Casualty
- Receive Demands
- Process Demands
- Order Materials

- Receive Materials
- Assemble Mandroid
- Test Mandroid
- Coordinate Pickup
- ....

The Wizdom facilitator then asks the team, *"What overall operational activity would you say encompasses each of these activities listed?"* The team comes up with an overall encompassing activity that will become the activity name of IDEF0's highest level model activity:

A0 MANAGE BORN JOINT COMBAT READY MANDROID SUPPORT.

Experienced with the IDEF0 activity modeling methodology, Wizdom facilitators work with the team to simplify the activity list to 3-6 main activities that describe the high-level operations taking place under the A0 MANAGE BORN JOINT COMBAT READY MANDROID SUPPORT activity. The team agrees on the following high-level indented list:

- A0 MANAGE BORN JOINT COMBAT READY MANDROID SUPPORT
    - A1 MANAGE DEMANDS
    - A2 ASSEMBLE MANDROIDS
    - A3 TEST MANDROIDS
    - A4 SCHEDULE PICKUP

The Wizdom facilitator directs the Wizdom analyst to open up the Process*Works*! IDEF0 modeling application and projects the application on the overhead screen for all to see. The team sees the beginning activity structure of what is to become the *'OV-5 Operational Activity Model'* that includes the purpose and viewpoint taken from the *AV-1*.

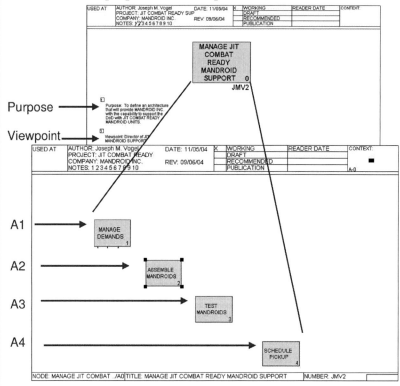

Figure 8.7 MANDROID OV-5 Creation Process

The process for completing the *OV-5* has only just begun. Many more facilitation sessions with the project team will take place before the *OV-5* will be considered complete. In fact, building the *OV-5* using IDEF0 will be complemented with considerable time and investment by MANDROID INC., because of the considerable amount of value that comes with a complete accurate IDEF0 model. With every facilitation session a new level of detailed composition will be identified. For each activity, the Wizdom facilitator will lead the team to identify further the sub activities and their corresponding inputs, outputs, controls, and mechanisms (ICOMs) as well as the Key Performance Indicators (KPIs) and Key Performance Parameters (KPPs).

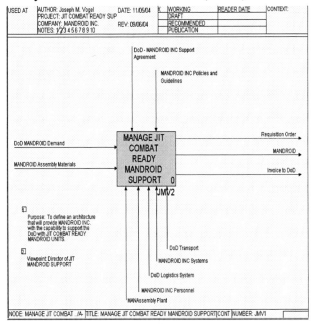

Figure 8.8 MANDROID OV-5 A-0

This highly detailed analysis will result in an updated *AV-2 Integrated Dictionary* as well as a new IDEF0 DoDAF work product known as the *OV-5: Operational Activity Model.* The highest level *OV-5* IDEF0diagrams (with ICOMs) developed by the team are displayed.

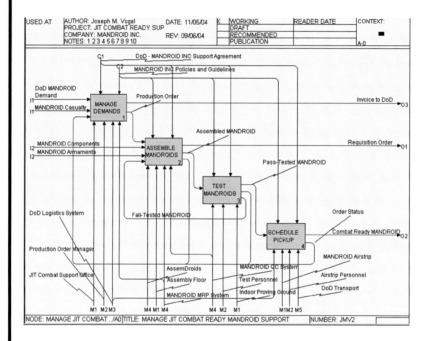

Figure 8.9 MANDROID OV-5 A0

The number of diagrams in the OV-5 continues to grow until the team proves to itself that it understands the MANDROID purpose. The project team continues to drill down on each box to identify sub activities and their supporting ICOMs. The facilitator will ensure that no turn shall be left unstoned during this endeavor, and will diligently carry this discovery process through until it is no longer necessary to decompose an activity.

During the discovery session a team member asks, "I know we are building our *OV-5* in IDEF0, but when are we going to start building the UML Use Cases and Process Flows?"

The Wizdom facilitator says, "We have been building them all along," and gestures to the analyst.

The analyst directs the group's attention to the screen. "The IDEF0 software converts the IDEF0 diagram, into a UML Use Case with the touch of a button!"

The UML Use Case equivalents display on the screen. The group is impressed.

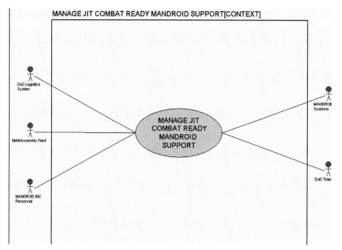

Figure 8.10 OV-5 Use Case

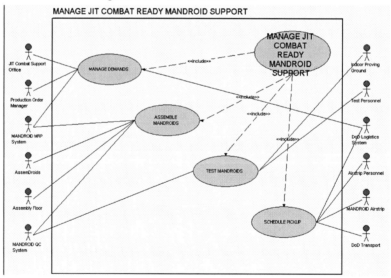

Figure 8.11 Use Case for the A0

This can be done because there is a correlation between a specific IDEF0 graphic diagram and a specific UML Use Case. Scenarios can be in IDEF0 text diagrams.

The facilitator continues with the demonstration to include the creation of an *OV-5* UML process flow model. At the press of another button, the analyst exports activities into an MS VISIO application (a popular application for diagramming Rummler-Brache swim lane diagrams). The activities in their respective swim lanes appear on the screen.

The facilitator says, "What you see here are the activities, but without the flow (logic). We can derive many different kinds of flows based on these activities in their respective swim lanes. Let's work together to identify one of those flows."

Flow properties are entered into the IDEF0 tool so that they can be shown in the swim lane diagram including KPIs and KPPs as appropriate.

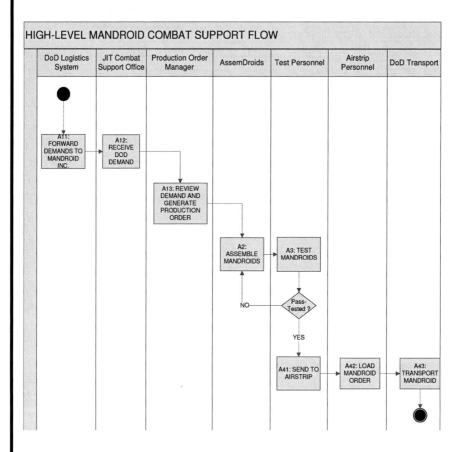

Figure 8.12 MANDROID Process Flow

Once again the team is impressed with the close correlations between IDEF0, UML Use Case, and process flow with little additional work.

The facilitator lets the group know that Step 2 facilitation sessions will start and stop all throughout the project as new *OV-5* activities and their respective ICOMS need to be identified. The facilitator also reminds them of the integrated dictionary in *AV-2* which will grow as the project continues forward.

The facilitator stresses to the group how important step 2 is in the Minimalist Methodology. This step provides a foundation from which all other steps can take place. It identifies a decomposition of activities, people, systems, information, and the rules and policies between them. The facilitator assures to the group that the upfront time and investment spent on this step will certainly reduce the time and rework on the steps to follow.

The analyst finishes the Step 2 facilitation sessions by uploading the *OV-1* and *OV-5* work products and related files up to the DoDAF project management tool for access and review by all members on the team.

In the next step, the team will begin to identify relationships between the people, data, and systems that will support MANDROID INC.'s ability to provide BORN JOINT COMBAT READY MANDROIDs to the DoD.

STEP 3: BUILD ORGANIZATIONAL RELATIONSHIP CHARTS, LOGICAL / PHYSICAL DATA MODELS, and SYSTEM FUNCTIONALITY DESCRIPTIONS

In steps 1 and 2, the team identified people, data, and systems that will provide BORN JOINT COMBAT READY MANDROIDs to the DoD. What was not identified in these steps were the relationships among people, data and systems. In the early stages of the project, the facilitator was able to obtain from MANDROID INC., a supporting personnel structure. Although MANDROID INC. has a larger support structure including personnel from sales, marketing, accounting, and design, the facilitator will limit the structure to those directly involved in providing BORN JOINT COMBAT READY MANDROIDS. This structure will become known as the '*OV-4: Organizational Relationships Chart.*'

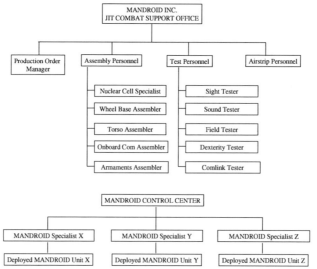

Figure 8.13 Organizational Relationships Chart

The facilitator leads the team through a review that includes all the ICOMs found on each *OV-5* IDEF0 diagram. The team identifies data entities, their attributes, and relationships, as they exist with other data entities in the *OV-5*. The analyst utilizes a FIPS compliant IDEF1X tool to capture data attributes and their relationships. When the team finishes with this review, they will have a work product in an IDEF1X format known as the *'OV-7: Logical Data Model'* including the business rules of operations.

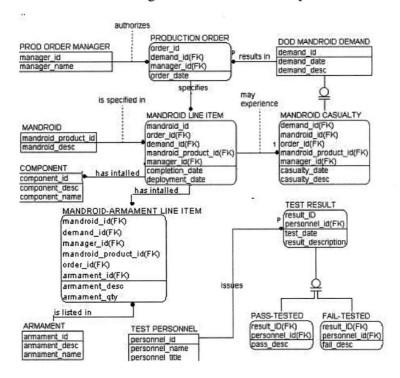

Figure 8.14 Logical Data Model

As the project continues, and additional systems are identified in *OV-5*, the facilitator will work with the teams to better understand the workflows between systems. By reviewing the *mechanism* ICOMs in the *OV-5* along with the *input* and *output* ICOMs, the team will be able to show these relationships in what is to become the '*SV-4: Systems Functionality Description.*'

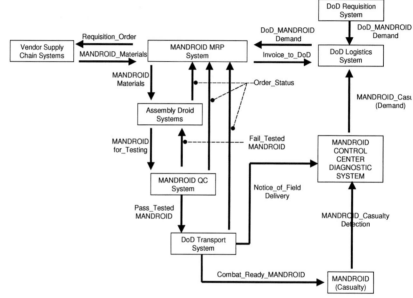

Figure 8.15 Systems Functionality Description

With a growing understanding of the operational and systems data relationships, the facilitator works with the MANDROID INC. IT personnel to build a data model that will be carried through to the end of the project and into the implementation phases of the system. This product will become one that is the most representative to the actual system design in the DoDAF. This will be a product that describes as much detail as possible on the MANDROID INC., system data elements exchanged between MANDROID INC., vendors, and DoD systems. The facilitator works with the team to include system elements such as 'DoD Transport,' 'QC Test Sensor,' and 'Assembly Droid' to the IDEF1X *OV*-7 logical model. There will be many more system elements added to this model as the *OV-7* will evolve into what becomes known as the '*SV-11: Physical Schema*'.

Figure 8.16 Physical Schema

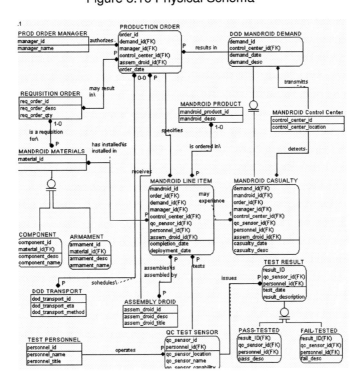

This step has focused primarily on understanding the data attributes and relationships with other data and system elements. As the team progresses through the other steps in the methodology, new data elements, relationships, and systems will be identified. In these cases, the *OV-4*, *OV-7*, *SV-4* and the *SV-11* will be updated respectively.

The analyst finishes Step 3 facilitation sessions by uploading the *OV-4*, *OV-7*, *SV-4* and the *SV-11* work products and related files up to the DoDAF*Live*! for access and review by all members on the team.

In the next step, the team will begin to identify operational and systems events that cause the people, data, and systems to exchange information in support of MANDROID INC.'s ability to provide BORN JOINT COMBAT READY MANDROIDs to the DoD.

STEP 4: BUILD OPERATIONAL EVENT TRACE DESRIPTION and SYSTEM EVENT TRACE DESCRIPTION

In this step, the facilitator will lead the team through various scenarios that will help describe how the architecture will behave based on operational and system events that take place.

One obvious scenario is to describe the high level operational events and information exchanges that take place between MANDROID INC., and the DoD when a MANDROID casualty is detected.

The team will utilize the *OV-1, OV-5, OV-4,* and *OV-7* work products to create the '*OV-6c Operational Event-Trace Description*'.

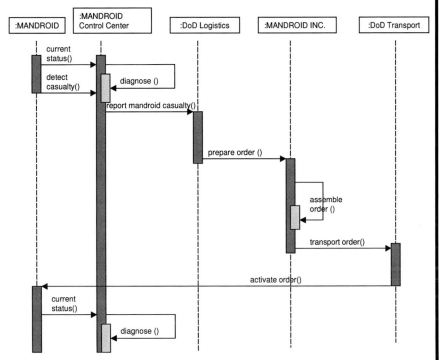

Figure 8.17 Operational Event-Trace Description

As the OV-5, SV-4, and SV-11 are developed, system data and relationships become better understood. With this understanding the team wants to expand its OV-6c scenario to include system elements such as 'MRP Order,' 'Assembly Droid,' and 'QC Sensor' system elements. With these systems elements introduced to the OV-6c, they can produce what will become the '*SV-10c: Systems-Event Trace Description.*'

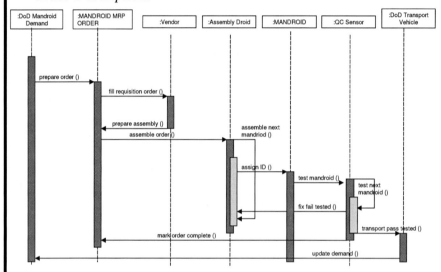

Figure 8.18 Systems Event-Trace Description

The team described how the system will behave based on the operational and system events that took place over a period of time. These diagrams help the team understand the behaviors, events, and timelines that are expected.

The analyst finishes Step 4 facilitation sessions by uploading the *OV-6c*, and the *SV-10c* work products and related files up to the DoDAF project management system for access and review by all members on the team.

STEP 5: BUILD OPERATIONAL INFORMATIONAL EXCHANGE MATRIX

The team now has several graphic representations that accurately describe the people, data, and systems of the architecture. Step 5 puts this information into a tabular format that can be quickly referenced in terms of *"who* exchanges *what* information, with *whom*, *why* the information is necessary, and *how* the information exchange must occur." [CJCSI 6212.01B, 2000] The team reviews its work products to produce what will become the *'OV-3: Operational Information Exchange Matrix.'*

Need line	Info Ex ID	Mission / Scenario	Trigger Event	Timeliness	Sending OP Node	Receiving OP Node
MANDROID Casualty	1	MANAGE DEMANDS	Upon detection of Casualty on the battlefield	Immediate	MANDROID Control Center	DoD Satellite
MANDROID Casualty via Satellite	2	MANAGE DEMANDS	Upon transmission arrival	Immediate	DoD Satellite	Defense Logistics System
DoD MANDROID Demand	3	MANAGE DEMANDS	Upon transmission arrival	Immediate	Defense Logistics System	MANDROID MRP System
Notice of Demand	4	MANAGE DEMANDS	Upon processed demand	Immediate	MANDROID MRP System	Production Order Manager
Authorized Order	5	MANAGE DEMANDS	Upon review of demand	Immediate	Production Order Manager	MANDROID MRP System
Requisition Order	6	ASSEMBLE MANDROIDS	Identification of need for material	Immediate	MANDROID MRP System	Vendor Supply Chain Systems
MANDROID Materials	7	ASSEMBLE MANDROIDS	Upon receipt of material	Immediate	Vendor Supply Chain Systems	MANDROID MRP System
MANDROID Materials	8	ASSEMBLE MANDROIDS	Upon receipt of material	Immediate	MANDROID MRP System	Assembly Droids
MANDROID for Testing	9	TEST MANDROIDS	Upon completion of assembly	24 hours	Assembly Droids	Test Personnel
Pass_Tested MANDROID	10	SCHEDULE PICKUP	Upon receiving pass-test status	JIT	Test Personnel	Dod Transport

Figure 8.19 Operational Information Exchange Matrix

This step also describes architecture conformance rules. The facilitator points out to the team that the products completed so far document the structure of the architecture, but what it hasn't documented yet is what the architecture *must* or *cannot* do. However, with the team's investment of time and resources while developing the *OV-5* from Step 2, the team's work on documenting these constraints will be minimal. This is due in part because the IDEF0 methodology used to build the *OV-5* calls for identifying controls –an ICOM constraint that dictates what activities *must* or *cannot* do. The team reviews the control arrows from the *OV-5* as well as contracts with DoD and vendors to build what will become the '*OV-6a: Operational Rules Model.*'

OPERATIONAL RULES:
1) MANDROID INC. must fill an order within 24 hours of receiving a DoD Demand.

2) MANDROID Control Centers are owned and operated by DoD personnel.

3) MANDROID units suffer casualties on the battlefield and must be re-supplied immediately. Casualties are detected by MANDROID unit diagnostic tools at MANDROID Control Centers.

4) MANDROID units are equipped with a low-yield nuclear core weapon. Battlefield commanders alone possess the serial code keys necessary to employ this weapon.

5) Assembly droids in combination with assembly personnel are used to assemble MANDROID units.

6) MANDROID INC. is supported by a system of vendors that makes up its MANDROID supply chain.

7) The DoD is entirely responsible for the pickup and transportation of orders off the MANDROID INC. premises.

8) The MANDROID INC. airstrip is maintained and secured by MANDROID INC. personnel for DoD pickup schedules.

Figure 8.20 Operational Rules Model

The example for this step, describes in detail both the information exchanges and rules by which the architecture will operate. These work products will provide business and IT personnel with a place of reference where, with the proper automated tools, they can update data and business rules across the architecture.

The analyst finishes Step 5 sessions by uploading the *OV-3*, and the *SV-10c* work products and related files to the DoDAF Project Management system for access and review by all members on the team.

STEP 6: BUILD OPERATIONAL STATE TRANSITION DESCRIPTION and SYSTEMS STATE TRANSITION DESCRIPTION

In the OV-6c and SV-10c the team documented a time-line of events that affected operational and system data. These documents only tell half the story in describing the lifecycle of a data element. The team sets out to describe the other half of the story by identifying the 'states' of significant operational and system data. By identifying these states, the team will also identify the operations required to change a data element's state from one state to another. Of the many operational data elements that exist in the architecture, the team chooses to model the state transitions of the MANDROID data element. This model is the '*OV-6b: Operational State Transition Description.*'

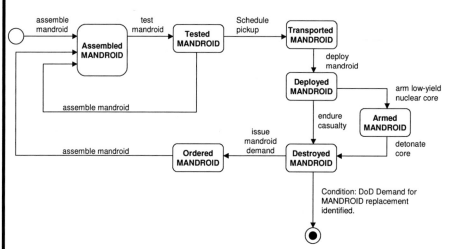

Figure 8.21 Operational State Transition Description

The team reviews its OV-6b and decides to dig deeper into the 'Tested MANDROID' state to identify the system's participation in the events and conditions that are taking place. They build what is to become one of many '*SV-10b System State Transition Description*' diagrams.

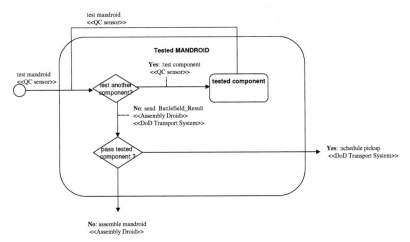

Figure 8.22 System State Transition Description

The team has described an operational and a system state transition. There are other state transitions that the team will need to review. For example, the transitions of a Purchase Order as it goes from being a DoD Demand, to being completely filled upon the event of a DoD scheduled pickup.

The team will also dig deeper into the cause and affect of these transitions to see the underlying system components that affect these states. These diagrams will help complete the lifecycle story of a data element. The IT personnel can use the SV-10c to design and implement a more accurate system.

The analyst finishes Step 6 by uploading the *OV-6b*, and the *SV-10b* work products and related files to the DoDAF *Project*

Management system for access and review by all team members.

STEP 7: BUILD OPERATIONS NODE CONNECTIVITY DIAGRAM

During the project, the team decided that it needed an overall view of the organizations and the information that flowed between them. The facilitator pulls out an *OV-4*, and an *OV-5*. The OV-4 shows some of the MANDROID INC. reporting hierarchy and the OV-5 illustrate the activities and information flows within this hierarchy. Taking elements from both, the team is able to construct what will become the *'OV-2: Operations Node Connectivity Diagram.'*

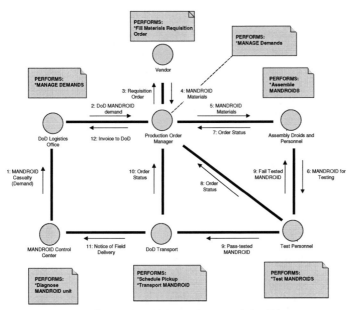

Figure 8.23 Operations Node Connectivity Diagram

This step essentially turned the *OV-5* inside out to show information flows between *OV-5* IDEF0 mechanisms (operational nodes). Although it is not required, but allowable, the team placed notes besides each node to indicate what activities that mechanism performs as well as show a sequence of flows between them.

The analyst finishes Step 7 by uploading the *OV-2* and related files to the Project Management system for access and review by all members on the team.

STEP 8: BUILD SYSTEMS INTERFACE DESCRIPTION (COMPONENTS)

In the previous step, the team built a high-level diagram of the operational nodes and the information flows that took place between them. Recall that in Step 2, that *OV-5* construction is ongoing as the team decomposes the IDEF0 operational activities into the lowest level of details necessary, but no more than.

Because of IDEF0's hierarchical nature, it will be at these lowest levels of detail where high-level mechanisms (operational nodes) become broken down into its component system parts. At these lower levels, the composition of the team will include IT personnel who are familiar with the technologies that support these activities. The team will see the evolving decomposition from nodes, to systems, to software modules and interfaces. The team has identified a need to map how these modules and interfaces work together by creating the '*SV-1: Systems Interface Description (Components)*' diagram.

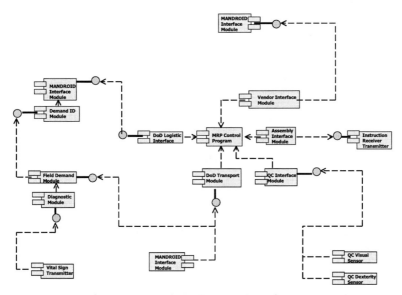

Figure 8.24 Systems Interface Description (Components)

In this step, the team used the lowest level activity models of the *OV-5* to drive out the low-level software components used to support the framework. IT personnel from all disciplines were included in the construction of this model to ensure that all system's interfaces have been defined. Building these kinds of diagrams will help the team - especially the IT personnel- identify missing interfaces and software components. The analyst finishes Step 8 by uploading the *SV-1* and related files to the Project Management system for access and review by all members on the team

STEP 9: BUILD FUNCTION, TRACEABILITY and DATA EXCHANGE MATRICES

The team recognizes a need to add more value to the component diagram drawing correlations between operational activities and system components. Step 5, put this information into a tabular format that depicted the mapping of these activities, to need lines and system functions. The team begins this step by identifying OV-5 IDEF0 functions and systems to build a matrix which is the '*SV-5: Operational Activity to Systems Function Traceability Matrix.*'

SYSTEMS SV-1/2		PROGRAM MODULES	Manage Demand	Assemble MANDROIDS	Test MANDROIDS	Schedule Pickup
MANDROID MRP SYSTEM		MRP Control Program	●	●	●	●
		Vendor Interface Module	●	●		
		Assembly Interface Module	●	●		
		QC Interface Module	●			
		DoD Transport Module	●			●
		DoD Logistics Interface Module	●			●
VENDOR SUPPLY SYSTEM		MANDROID Interface Module	●	●		
ASSEMBLY SYSTEM		Instruction Receiver		●		
		Instruction Transmitter		●		
MANDROID QC System		QC Dexterity Sensor			●	
		QC Visual Sensor			●	

Figure 8.25 Operational Activity to Systems Function Matrix

From this matrix, there is a clear understanding of what software modules contribute to which operational processes. This matrix also shows which systems these modules are associated with. The *SV-5* addresses the functional and operational traceability aspects of this step. The team now needs to address the data exchange aspects between system functions - the '*SV-6: Systems Data Exchange Matrix.*'

IER #	Sender	Receiver	Content	Media	Format	Freq.	Time	Throughput
1	Diagnostic Module	Field Demand Module	MANDROID casualty	DDE	SATMAT	N/A	5sec	1GB/sec
2	Field Demand Module	Demand ID Module	flag for MANDROID replacement	N/A	SATMAT	N/A	5sec 5sec	100mb/sec
3	Demand ID Module	DoD Logistic Interface	DoD demand	SAT-Trans	SATMAT	N/A	5sec	1GB/sec
4	DoD Logistic Interface	MRP Control Program	Production Order	SLS	Voice, data,	N/A	N/A	1GB/sec
5	MRP Control Program	Vendor Interface Module	Material Requisition Order	DDE	data	N/A	N/A	100mb/sec
6	Vendor Interface Module	MANDROID Interface Module	Material Requisition Order	DDE	Voice, data,	N/A	10sec	100mb/sec
7	MRP Control Program	Assembly Interface Module	Production Order	N/A	SATMAT	N/A	10sec	100mb/sec
8	Assembly Interface Module	Instruction Receiver	Operation request	N/A	data	N/A	N/A	100mb/sec
9	QC Visual Sensor	QC Interface Module	Test Status	OLS	data	N/A	N/A	100mb/sec
10	QC Dexterity Sensor	QC Interface Module	Test Status	OLS	data	N/A	10sec	100mb/sec
…n	…	…	…	…	…	…	…	…

Figure 8.26 Systems Data Exchange Matrix

The *SV-5* and *SV-6* work products from this step will provide IT personnel with the specific Input/Output (IO) performance requirements and expectations that are necessary in developing and maintaining program module components.

The analyst finishes Step 9 by uploading the *SV-5, SV-6,* and related files to the Project Management system for access and review by all members on the team

STEP 10: BUILD SYSTEMS INTERFACE DESCRIPTION (DEPLOYMENT)

This step is in a way a continuation of Step 8. This step graphically associates system components with the actual systems themselves. This step adds value to the SV-1 by illustrating the physical deployment between systems and program modules. This added value to the SV-1 will be the '*SV-1: System Interface Description (Deployment)*' diagram.

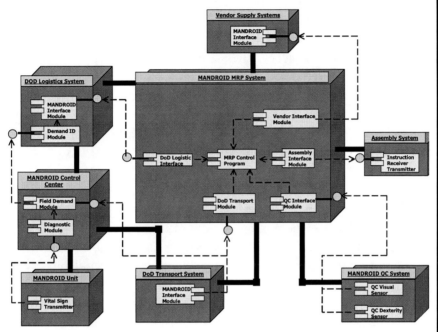

Figure 8.27 Systems Interface Description (Deployment)

Value is added to the *SV-1* component diagram with these new graphical deployment representations. This diagram provides business and IT personnel with a tool for discussing future systems, their components, and how they will fit in with the current architecture.

The analyst finishes Step 10 by uploading an updated *SV-1* and related files to the Project Management system for access and review by all members on the team

STEP 11: BUILD AND MAINTAIN THE TECHNICAL STANDARDS PROFILE

The final step to the minimalist methodology takes place all throughout the project. In steps 1 through 10, project teams will have at least one member who is knowledgeable of the conventions and standards that are to be used in building the systems that will support the MANDROID INC., architecture. These individuals will most likely be IT personnel, and more involved in the creation of SV work products.

As the team completes a work product, the analyst will work with the IT personnel to identify and document standards that will apply to new system elements that were identified in the work product. Overarching reference models such as the Joint Technical Architecture (JTA), OMB's TRM, DoD's TRM and their respective services can be used. However, the analyst will pick and choose those reference models that best meet the needs of the architecture.

In this scenario, the analyst has chosen the JTA reference to document these standards. These standards extensive with detail will be documented in MANDROID INC.'s *'TV-1: Technical Standards Profile.'*

JTA SERVICE AREA	SERVICE	JTA STANDARD AND SOURCE DOCUMENT
Information Modeling, Metadata, and Information Exchange Standards		
	Activity Modeling	<u>IDEF0</u>:IEEE 1320.1:1998, IEEE Standard for Functional Modeling Language-Syntax and Semantics for IDEF0. [SUNSET] This standard will be deleted when version 2.0 of the DoD Architecture Framework is released.
	Data Modeling	<u>IDEF1X</u>: FIPS PUB 184, Integration Definition for Information Modeling (IDEF1X), December 1993.
	Object Modeling	<u>UML:</u>Object Management Group (OMG) Unified Modeling Language (UML) Specification,Version 1.4, September 2001.
	DoD Data Architecture Implementation	-none mandated
	Information Exchange	<u>BIT ORIENTED:</u>MIL-STD-6016B, Tactical Digital Information Link (TADIL) J Message Standard, 1 August 2002. [SUNSET] This standard will be deleted with the delivery of efficient XML-based message services from GES. <u>VARIABLE MESSAGE FORMAT:</u> (VMF), Technical Interface Design Plan (Test Edition) Reissue 5,18 January 2002. [SUNSET] This standard will be deleted with the delivery of efficient XML-based message services from GES.
Human-Computer Interface Standards		
	General User Interface Design	(See User Interface Services and Operating System Services)

Figure 8.28 TV-1 Partial Technical Standards Profile

CONCLUSION

The team completes steps 1 through 11 and now has a minimal number of architecture work products that make them compliant with the DoDAF.

The team completes its work and its progress has been recorded in DoDAF*Live*!

MANDROID INC. presents this architecture and wins a new contract with the DoD.

Summary and References

Now this is not the end. It is not even the beginning of the end. But it is, perhaps, the end of the beginning.

- SIR WINSTON CHURCHILL

DoD seeks continuous Enterprise Transformation. This is the same goal as the Federal Government and indeed the siren call of organizations around the world.

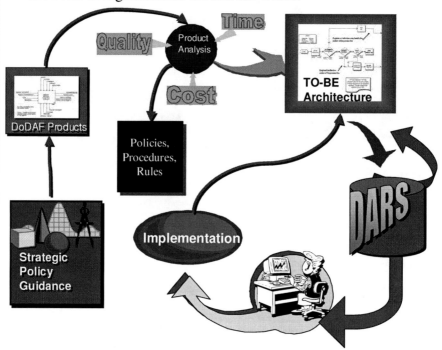

Figure S.1 Enterprise Transformation

Perhaps the biggest understatement of the Rumsfeld Pentagon was when he was quoted as saying:

*"Substantial change will be required within DoD's business management communities to achieve the Business Management Modernization Program (BMMP) objectives - **<u>BMMP represents one of the largest business transformation efforts undertaken to date.</u>**"*

This reference is to the Business Management Modernization Program (BMMP) that has been previously mentioned. These authors know of nothing bigger ever attempted anywhere.

And, this is the tip of the Iceberg.

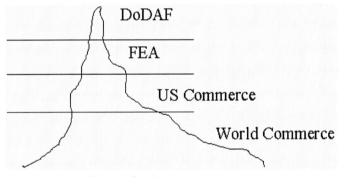

Figure S.2 Iceberg

Icebergs have only about 10% of their volume above the surface. 80% to 90% is below the surface. The metaphor here is that the DoDAF is merely the tip – or less of the EA. Navigate diligently.

References

Chapter One

Dennis E. Wisnosky, Rita Feeney, <u>BPR Wizdom – A Practical Guide to Business Process Reengineering Project Management</u>, Wizdom Press, Naperville, Illinois, 2001
http://www.omg.org/docs/omg/03-06-01.pdf
http://www.cs.vu.nl/~henk/research/via/0308so/2-method-support-stakeh-orient-viewpoints-v01.pdf
http://www.opengroup.org/architecture/togaf/
http://www.dstc.edu.au/Research/Projects/ODP/ref_model.html
http://www.oasis-open.org/committees/tc_home.php?wg_abbrev=bcm
http://www.ichnet.org/SAIL/SAIL%20FAQ.doc
http://www.bpmi.org/
http://www.feapmo.gov/
Fred Stein, David Alberts, John Garstka, *Network Centric Warfare: Developing and Leveraging Information Superiority,* 2nd Edition (CCRP Publication Series), 1999.
http://public.afca.af.mil/Intercom/2004/MAY/StartingLineup.pdf
http://acc.dau.mil/simplify/ev.php?ID=22878_201&ID2=DO_TOPIC

- Industry Advisory Council Enterprise Architecture SIG, <u>Succeeding with Component-based Architectures – Draft</u>, 2002 http://www.enterprise-architecture.info/Images/Defence%20C4ISR/enterprise_architecture_reference_models_v0_8.pdf

Paul Strassman. *The Squandered Computer: Evaluation the Business Alignment of Information Technologies*. The Information Economics Press. New Canaan, CT, 1997

Dennis E. Wisnosky. *SoftLogic: Overcoming Funnel Vision*. Wizdom Systems, Inc., Naperville, IL, 1996.

Chapter Two

http://jitc.fhu.disa.mil/jitc_dri/jitc.html

Frederick Winslow Taylor. *The Principles of Scientific Management*. Dover Publications. New York, 1998.

Noel M. Tichy and Stratford Sherman. *Control Your Destiny or Someone Else Will: Lessons in Mastering Change.* Harper Business. New York, 1999.

http://www.geocities.com/Eureka/Enterprises/9942/managementpeterdrucker.html

Chapter Three

Frederick P. Brooks Jr. *The Mythical Man-Month: Essays on Software Engineering*. Addison Wesley. Reading, PA, 1995.

W. Edwards Deming. *Out of Crisis*. Massachusetts Institute of Technology. Cambridge, MA, 1986.

http://www.elec.york.ac.uk/visual/jar11/engineering/ndesmeth.html

Chapter Four

Steven C. Hill and Lee A. Robinson. *A Concise Guide to the IDEF0 Technique*. Enterprise Technology Concepts Press. Puyallup, WA, 1995

David A. Marca and Clement L. McGowan. *SADT: Structured Analysis and Design Technique*. McGraw-Hill. New York, 1987.

National Institute of Standards and Technology, U.S. Department of Commerce. Federal Information

Processing Standards Publications, December 21, 1993:
- *FIPS 183: Integration Definition for Function Modeling (IDEF 0)*
- *FIPS 184: Integration Definition for Information Modeling (IDEF 1X)*

Chapter Five

Alistair Cockburn, *Writing Effective Use Cases*, Pearson Education, New Jersey, 2001.

Eriksson, Hans-Erik, Penker, Magnus, <u>Business Modeling with UML – Business Patterns that Work</u>, John Wiley & Sons, Inc. New York, 2000

Rumbaugh, James, Jacobson, Ivar, Booch, Grady, <u>The Unified Modeling Language Reference Manual</u>, Addison-Wesley, Reading, Massachusetts, 1999

Schmuller, Joseph, Sams Teach Yourself UML in 24 Hours – Second Edition, Sams Publishing, Indianapolis, Indiana, 2002

Chapter Six

http://www.dodccrp.org/events/2004/CCRTS_San_Diego/CD/papers/208.pdf

http://www.dodccrp.org/events/2004/CCRTS_San Diego/CD/papers/208.pdf

http://akss.dau.mil/jsp/default.jsp

http://www.dtic.mil/whs/directives/corres/pdf2/d46305p.pdf - Establishes the Net-Ready Key Performance Parameter (NR-KPP) to assess net-ready attributes required for both the technical exchange of information and the end-to-end operational effectiveness of that exchange. The NR-KPP replaces the Interoperability KPP and incorporates net-centric concepts for achieving IT and NSS interoperability and supportability.

http://www.dtic.mil/cjcs_directives/cdata/unlimit/6212_01.pdf - Details the Net-Ready Key Performance Parameter (NR-KPP) in lieu of the Interoperability KPP (I KPP) discussed in CJCSI 3170.01C and CJCSM 3170.01.

DoD Instruction 5000.2, "Operation of the Defense Acquisition System," May 12, 2003

DoD Directive 8100.1, "Global Information Grid (GIG) Overarching Policy," September 19, 2002
DoD Instruction 4120.24, "Defense Standardization Program (DSP)," June 18, 1998

Section 133 of title 10, United States Code

DoD Directive 8500.1, "Information Assurance (IA)," October 24, 2002

DoD Instruction 8500.2, "Information Assurance (IA) Implementation," February 6, 2003

DoD Instruction 5200.40, "DoD Information Technology Security Certification and Accreditation Process (DITSCAP)," December 30, 1997

National Security Telecommunications and Information Systems Security Policy (NSTISSP) No. 11, "National Policy Governing the Acquisition of Information Assurance (IA) and IA-Enabled Information Technology (IT) Products," June 2003 [1]

DCI Directive 6/3, "Protecting Sensitive Compartmented Information Within Information Systems," June 5, 1999

Office of the Intelligence Community (IC) Chief Information Officer (CIO), "Top Secret/Sensitive Compartmented Information and Below Interoperability (TSABI) Policy," v4.20, November 24, 2003 [2]

Unpowered Jet Airliner Landings
http://airsafe.com/events/noengine.htm -- Revised: 25 February 2004

Robert S. Kaplan and David P. Norton. *The Balanced Scorecard: Translating Strategy into Action*. Harvard Business School. Boston, 1996.

Tom Pryor and Julie Sahm. *Using Activity Based Management for Continuous Improvement*. ICMS. Arlington, TX, 1994.

Wizdom Systems, Inc. *Manufacturing Enterprise Reference Model: Continuous Business Process Improvement is Model Driven*. Wizdom Systems, Inc. Naperville, IL, 1999.

Chapter Seven

Little Eye is a concept that I first saw developed by Steven H. Dam, Ph.D. for a DoDAF training course hosted by Technology Training Corporation. Dr. Dam is the President and Founder of the Systems and Proposal Engineering Company (SPEC) and SPEC Software, both based in Marshall, VA. Dr. Dam used Little Eye as a class room exercise. The embellished the concept to encompass every DoDAF product.

Framework for Managing Process Improvement. Command, Control, Communication & Intelligence. Department of Defense, 12/15/94.

Chapter Eight

Mandroid - *A humanoid robot; a robot in the shape of a person.* So says http://www.technovelgy.com/ct/content.asp?Bnum=612 The word appears to originate in a 1986 movie named "The Eliminators." Marvel Comics also used the name "Mandroid" to refer to an armored personal combat suit (this first showed up in Avengers #94, in December 1971). Justin Higgins gets his email at jlh@mandroid.com. It is used here with full attribution to anyone who claims ownership.

Appendix A

DoDAF Tools

As of this writing, there are 9 companies known to be actively working with DoD and its DARS support contractors on proving DoDAF product interchangeability. These are the companies included in this group.

Vendor	Software	Primary Function	Category	Download
Agilense www.agilense.com	EA WebModeler	Diagramming, Modeling, Analysis, Process	Modeling, Analysis, Program Management	Offer evals
Booz Allen Hamilton 703-882-2270 www.bah.com *did not respond to inquiry				
Computas 425-391-2000 http://www.computas.com/ *did not immediately respond to inquiry	Metis sales@computas.com	Simulation	Modeling	YES
Computas 425-391-2000 http://www.computas.com/ *did not immediately respond to inquiry	FrameSolution sales@computas.com	Workflow, Process	Project Management	NO

Vendor	Software	Primary Function	Category	Down load
IBM 800-426-7378 http://www-306.ibm.com/software/rational/ *did not respond to inquiry	Rational Rose ews@us.ibm.com			
IDS Scheer 248-356-9775 http://www.ids-scheer.com/	ARIS	Diagramming, Process, Workflow Simulation	Analysis, Simulation, Project Management	YES
Popkin 646-346-8500 http://www.popkin.com/products/system_architect.htm	SystemArchitect sales@popkin.com	Diagramming, Simulation		
Proforma 248-356-9775 http://www.proformacorp.com/index.asp	ProVison info@proformacorp.com or sales@proformacop.com	Analysis, Simulation	Modeling, Analysis, Simulation, Diagramming	YES
Schafer 703-558-7900 http://www.schaferdc.com/ *did not respond to inquiry				

Vendor	Software	Primary Function	Category	Download
Trident Systems Inc 703-691-7792 http://www.interchangese.com/	InterchangeSE InterchangeSE@tridsys.com	Process, Diagramming	Project Management, Simulation, Modeling, Diagramming, Analysis	NO
Vitech Corporation 703-883-2270 www.vitechcorp.com	CORE/COREsim info@vitechcorp.com	Workflow, Diagramming, Modeling, Analysis, Process, Simulation	Modeling, Diagramming, Simulation, Project Management	Upon Request
Wizdom Systems 630-357-3000 http://wizdom.com	Wizdom*Works!* robind@wizdom.com	Workflow, Process, Simulation, Analysis	Project Management, Modeling, Analysis	YES
Wizdom Systems 630-357-3000 http://wizdom.com	DoDAF*Live!* robind@wizdom.com	Process	Project Management	YES

**Information was gathered thru product research surveys and was not edited or altered.

Appendix B

Process Models to Data Models to Data Bases to Application Code

NIST HII Project report by Philip A. Olson, Jr., 10 April 1997
and updated by Les Sanders, 15 March 1999

The process of converting user requirements into a relational database has been time consuming and frustrating for both the designers and the users for years. That has all changed in the recent past. We now have the capability to develop functionally validated activity models and logical data models using graphical support applications in time frames that were considered impossible in the recent past. These tools capture the requirements information provided by the organization's functional experts, transform it into views with which management can work, relate it to the logical data model developed by the information modeling team, and provide interfaces to the analysis tools and database management systems needed to evaluate the information and store the data instances. This paper describes this process in detail.

The first step in the process is to capture the requirements information from the users. This is generally done in a cooperative workshop environment and results in an IDEF0 model which has a context diagram to set the stage for further decomposition of the activities into their component parts down to the level needed to understand and refine the activities. Figure B.1 shows a context diagram.

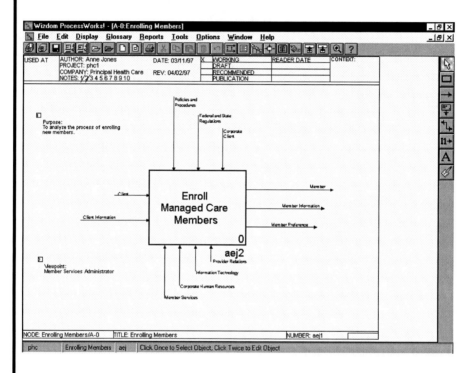

Figure B.1: Context Diagram

The context diagram activity is decomposed into 3 to 6 subprocesses, each of which is decomposed into 3 to 6 subprocesses and so on until the functional users are satisfied that they do not need any additional detail. It is critical during this process that the activities and ICOMs displayed in the model are defined and that consensus be achieved on the definitions. Figure B.2 displays the subprocesses generated from the breakdown of the context diagram.

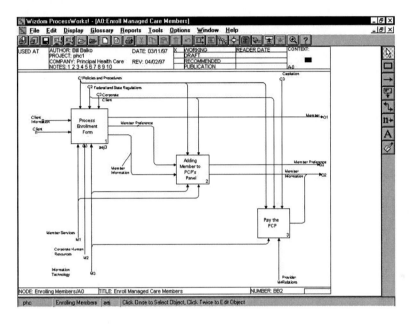

Figure B.2: First Level Subprocesses from the Context Diagram

Once the ICOMs and activities have been defined and the interrelationships have been drawn into the model, work on the analysis of the model can begin. WizdomWorks! provides interfaces to several tools as shown in Figure B.3.

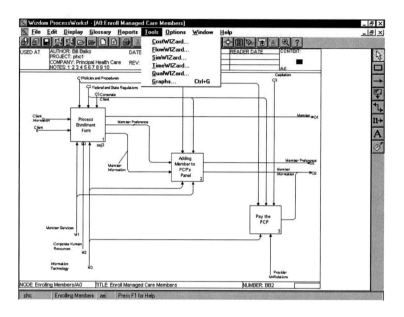

Figure B.3: WizdomWorks! Tools

Each of the analysis tools provides a unique view of the information in the activity model and enables management to make its decisions based on analysis rather than pure guesswork. For example, the CostWizard can help to identify non-value added activities and their associated costs which can be used to convince management to get rid of some of their sacred cows which can't be cost justified. The other interfaces provide similar capabilities.

Because the Wizdom activity and data modeling tools share the same glossary database, definitions for the ICOMs which were developed during the activity modeling work can be used in the development of the logical data model. A small part of a logical data model which was developed in support of a medical function is displayed in Figure B.4.

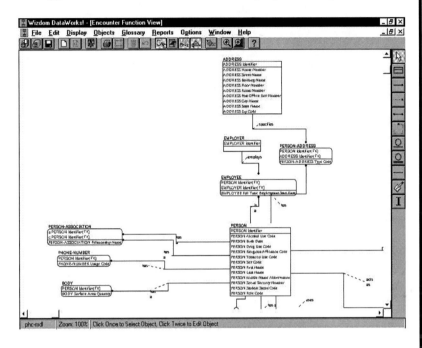

Figure B.4: Logical Data Model Excerpt

The logical model displayed in Figure B.4 shows many of the salient features of standard IDEF1x data models. Boxes with square corners represent independent entities while those with rounded corners represent dependent entities. The name of the entity is shown above the box and the attributes of the entity are displayed inside the box. The attributes that are listed above the horizontal line inside the box are the key attributes that are used to uniquely identify instances of the entity. The attributes that are listed below the horizontal line represent non-key characteristics of the entity. Every entity must have at least one key attribute but may have as many non-key attributes as are necessary to capture the important information about the entity. Identifying relationships (those which provide foreign keys to the entity at the end with the dot) are represented by solid lines and are labeled with the name of the relationship. Relationships are read from the end without the dot to the end with the dot. For example, EMPLOYER employs EMPLOYEE and PERSON is EMPLOYEE. Notice that the key of EMPLOYEE has two parts. The first part migrates to the EMPLOYEE entity from the EMPLOYER entity along the **employs** relationship and the second part migrates from the PERSON entity along the **is** relationship.

Once the logical model is developed, it is now possible to export the entity and attribute structure in the form of SQL statements which create table structures in an Oracle database. The SQL export is an option of the **Reports** drop down menu. See Figure B.5.

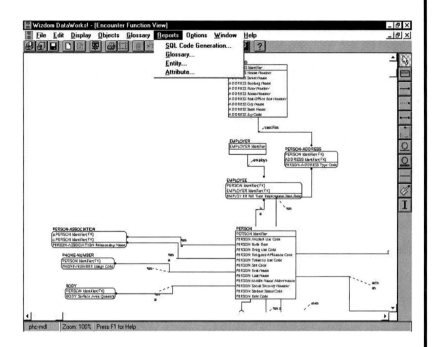

Figure B.5: SQL Code Export

A sample of the exported SQL from the above model is provided in Figure B.6.

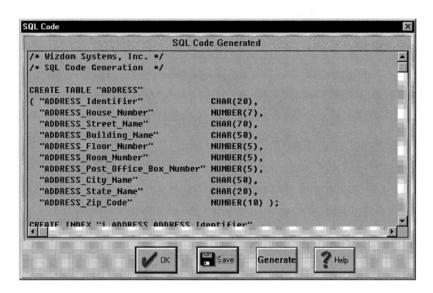

Figure B.6: SQL Code Generation

The SQL script can be saved as a file and then the file is executed from within an SQL*Plus session after the Oracle database has been started and SQL*DBA has been connected internally. Execution of the script causes Oracle to create the appropriate tables with the specified columns and to set up the relational constraints linking the tables together. Once the tables are created in the Oracle database, they can be loaded with data and used. The string data type **varchar (20)** is the default type for each column created. This default can be overridden from within the DataWorks! program prior to generating the SQL script which is used to create the tables. It must be done on a case-by-case basis just as would have to be done if the create statements were all generated by hand instead of by the software. In Figure B.7 below, the type is shown as CHAR(20) for the ADDRESS Identifier. This is the **Attribute Edit** dialog box, which is available from the **Objects** drop down menu.

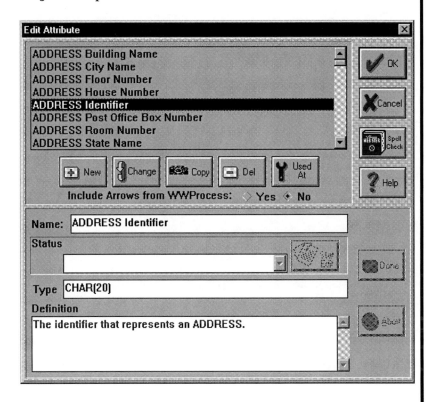

Figure B.7: Editing the Attribute Type

After the data tables are generated in the Oracle database, the data values can be loaded in a variety of ways depending on how they are collected.

A new feature of WizdomWorks! enables users to create databases directly from the generated SQL code. Figure B.8 shows the dialog that is presented to the user if they select the "Generate" button in Figure B.6. Through this dialog, DataWorks! can generate any installed ODBC (Open Data Base Connectivity) compatible database.

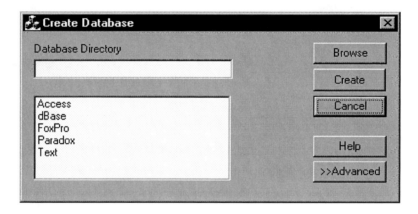

Figure B.8: Generating an ODBC Database

Appendix C

Glossary of Terms

Activity
A process, function or task that occurs over time and has recognizable results. Activities combine to form business processes.

Activity Based Costing (ABC)
An accounting technique that allows an enterprise to determine the actual costs associated with each product and service produced by that enterprise without regard to the organizational structure of the enterprise. (See Wizdom's ABC Costing Training Course and Wizdom's BPR Software tool, CostWIZ.)

Activity Model
A graphic representation of a business process that exhibits the activities and their interdependencies that make up the business process to any desired level of detail. An activity model reveals the interactions between activities in terms of inputs and outputs while showing the controls placed on each activity and the types of resources assigned to each activity. (Wizdom offers a training course in IDEF Activity modeling and ProcessWorks! process and activity modeling software.)

Actor
A specialization of a resource needed to perform an activity.

Annual Operating Plan
This plan features an organization's implementing actions and specifies (a) how the unit will contribute directly to the achievement of the strategic initiatives over the next year, and (b) how it will achieve its unit Performance Goals. Annual operating plans are carried down to each individual (or team) within each unit through personal plans and Performance Goals.

Application Program Interface
A set of callable routines that a programmer uses to interact with an application.

Architecture
The organizational structure of a system or CSCI, identifying its components, their interfaces, and a concept of execution among them.

AS-IS Model
A model that represents the current stage of the organization modeled, without any specific improvements included. <a href="bprsoftware.htm">WizdomWorks! BPR Software helps you create accurate AS-IS models.<p>

Attribute

A property or characteristic that is common to some or all of the instances of an entity. An attribute represents the use of a domain in the context of an entity.

BPMI
The Business Process Management Initiative is managed by BPMI.org which seeks to define open specifications, such as the Business Process Modeling Language (BPML), and the Business Process Query Language (BPQL), that will enable the standards-based management of e-Business processes with forthcoming Business Process Management Systems (BPMS), in much the same way SQL enabled the standards-based management of business data with off-the-shelf Database Management Systems (DBMS).

Baseline
The current condition that exists in a situation. Usually used to differentiate between a current and a future representation.

Benchmarking
A method of measuring processes against those of recognized leaders to establish priorities and targets leading to process improvement. It is undertaken by identifying strategies, customers, processes and costs to benchmark and their key characteristics; determining who to benchmark; collecting and analyzing data from direct contact, survey,

interviews, technical journals and advertisements; determining the "best of class" from each benchmark item identified; and evaluating the process in terms of improvement goals.

Best Practice
A way or method of accomplishing a business function or process that is considered to be superior to all other known methods.

Business Architecture Modernization (BAM, formerly called SBPR)
A contract vehicle sponsored by the Department of Defense. The contract provides business process reengineering support services focused on the higher order strategic and management assessment functions. Reengineering services include fully qualified BPR experts with functional knowledge in all aspects of process engineering, state-of-the-art analytical tools and time-tested methodologies for comprehensive process improvement.

Business Case
A structured proposal for business process improvement that functions as a decision package for enterprise leadership. A business case includes an analysis of business process needs or problems, proposed solution, assumptions and constraints, alternatives, life cycle costs, benefits/cost analysis and investment risk analysis. Within DoD, a business case is called a Functional Economic Analysis (FEA).

Business Objectives
Goals of the organization that can be measured in some quantitative way. (e.g., Decrease cost by 15%. Become the supplier with the lowest rate of returned products).

Business Process Improvement
The betterment of an organization's business practices through the analysis of activities to reduce or eliminate non-value added activities or costs, while at the same time maintaining or improving quality, productivity, timeliness, or other strategic or business purposes as evidenced by measures of performance. Also called Functional Process Improvement. See Wizdom's BPR Software

Business Process Portal
A process portal focuses, or that is able to be focused, on solving a particular business problem or manage a particular business function. Business Process Portals bring the right information to the right people at the right time to help them get their work done.

Business Process Reengineering (BPR)
A structured approach by all or part of an enterprise to improve the value of its products and services while reducing resource requirements. The transformation of a business process to achieve significant levels of improvement in one or more performance measures relating to fitness for purpose, quality, cycle time, and cost by using the techniques of streamlining and removing added

activities and costs. Redesign projects typically take about six months to complete. Also referred to as Business Process Improvement (BPR), Business Process Redesign, and Functional Process Improvement. (See WizdomWorks! BPR Software, Wizdom BPR Consulting, and Wizdom BPR Training Courses.

C4ISR
DoD Command, Control, Communications, Computers, Intelligence, Surveillance, and Reconnaissance (C4ISR) Architecture Framework.

CADM
The All-DoD Core Architecture Data Model (CADM) defines the entities and relationships for architecture data elements. The CADM was developed cooperatively by representatives from the Office of the Secretary of Defense, Combatant Commands, Military Services, and Defense Agencies as the DoD standard architecture data model for Framework-based architecture data elements. [All-CADM, 200 3a, b, c] The CADM is built using the Integrated Definition for Data Modeling, IDEF1X [FIPS 184, 1993] methodology, notation, and forms. More than 95 percent of the entities and attributes from the CADM are approved as DoD architecture data standards. Using relational technology labels,

for example, the entities from the CADM provide specifications for tables in a database, and the CADM attributes provide

Cause and Effect Diagram (Ishikawa Fishbone)
This facilitation technique graphically displays a detailed list of causes related to a problem or conditions, for the purpose of discovering its root cause(s) and not just symptoms.

Wizdom's Process Analysis & Redesign training course teaches how to Identify problem causes and solutions with the Cause & Effect Diagram (Ishakawa fishbone).

Consolidated Tool Model
A consolidation of metamodels from the existing tools studied. We are seeking to define and build (as proof of concept) a better repository. We have collected the metamodels from several existing products. We are currently creating a Consolidated Tool Model by bringing these metamodels together in a single model representation. This Consolidated Tool model will provide us with the schema (data layout) for a Repository of existing tools. This Repository will grow as we add tools and as we define how to handle the rules and how they evolve into a knowledge store.

Continuous Process Improvement

A policy that encourages, mandates, and/or empowers employees to find ways to improve process and product performance measures on an ongoing basis.

Cross Functional Process Improvement
BPR with the goal of eliminating stove pipe operations Processes interact between functions as necessary to achieve business objectives. (*See Stove Pipe*).

Data
From Oracle publication on CASE metamodel defines database as: When an application is operating, the computer is manipulating information in the real world. (e.g., product descriptions, pricing information, customer details). This information is known as data.

Data Active
Information that has behavior knowledge so that its representation changes on the basis of the environment in which it is used.

Database
A collection of interrelated data, often with controlled redundancy, organized according to a schema to serve one or more applications.

Database Management Systems Object
A Database Management System (DMBS) that is encapsulated as an object or a component with a set of explicitly defined public methods or interfaces. Such a component could be used within a compatible component architecture (e.g., MS COM/DCOM/ActiveX, CORBA, Java Bean Enterprise architecture)

A DBMS such as Oracle7 or Oracle8 loosely defines internal structures it manages as entities or objects.

Data Model
From FIPS PUB 184: A graphical and textual representation of analysis that identifies the data needed by an organization to achieve its mission functions, goals, objectives, and strategies, and to manage and rate the organization. A data model identifies the entities, domains (attributes) and relationships (or associations) with other data, and provides the conceptual view of the data and the relationships among data.

Data Passive
Static information that represents something; that something is only known by the application which is responsible for interpreting its meaning.

Data Repository
A specialized database containing information about data

and data relationships. Used to provide a common resource of standard data elements and models.

DISA
Defense Information Systems Agency

Discounted Cash Flow
A method of performing an economic analysis that takes the time value of money into account. Used to remove interest rates and inflation factors from a calculation so that the results of analysis are comparable.

DoD
US Department of Defense

DoDAF
The Department of Defense (DoD) Architecture Framework (DoDAF), Version 1.0, defines a common approach for DoD architecture description development, presentation, and integration for both warfighting operations and business operations and processes. The Framework is intended to ensure that architecture descriptions can be compared and related across organizational boundaries, including Joint and multinational boundaries.

Domain
Oracle publication on CASE metamodel defines domain as:

1. A set of business validation rules, format constraints and other properties that apply to a group of attributes. For example, a list of values, a range, a qualified list or range or any combination of these.

2. *From FIPS PUB 184:* A named set of data values (fixed or possibly infinite in number) all of the same data type, upon which the actual value for an attribute instance is drawn. Every attribute must be defined on exactly one underlying domain. Multiple attributes may be based on the same underlying domain.

3. *From DISA/CIM:* A set of current and future systems that shares a set of common requirement, capabilities, and data. A logical grouping of related functions and objects. Often referred to as problem domain, problem space, or problem area.

Economic Analysis
A formal method of comparing two or more alternative ways of accomplishing a set objective, given a set of assumptions and constraints and the costs and benefits of each alternative, such that the analysis will indicate the optimum choice.

Enterprise
An organization that exists to perform a specific mission and achieve associated goals and objectives.

Entity
The representation of a set of real or abstract things (people, objects, places, events, ideas, combination of things, etc.) that are recognized as the same type because they share the same characteristics and can participate in the same relationships.

Event
A happening, the arrival of a significant point in time, a change in status of something or the occurrence of something external that causes the business to react.

Extensibility
It is often useful to add new elements, properties and associations into a BPR project Dictionary. This is achieved be a facility known as (user) extensibility.

Field
From Oracle CASE Dictionary Ref Guide: A means of implementing an item of data within a file. It can be in character, date, number or other format, and can be optional or mandatory.

File
From Oracle CASE Dictionary Ref Guide: A method of implementing part or all of a database.

Fixed Cost
A cost that does not vary with the amount or degree of production. The costs that remain if an activity or process stops.

Function
An action or activity proper to a person, a thing, or particular business unit within the organization. (e.g., Flying = function performed by an airline).

Functional Area
A grouping of actions or processes that is appropriate to or necessary for accomplishing a task or related tasks. These actions or activities may be organized on a small (micro) or large (macro) scale. E.G. Admissions includes functional areas of data entry and interviewing detainees. Admissions, Incarceration, Community Supervision, and Release are defined as functional areas of DPSCS in the Andersen report.

Functional Economic Analysis (FEA)
A technique for analyzing and evaluating alternative information system investments and management practices. Within DoD, FEA is a business case. Also, a document that contains a fully justified proposed improvement project with all supporting data.

Functional Process Improvement
A structured approach by all or part of an enterprise to improve the value of its products and services while

reducing resource requirements. Also referred to as business process improvement (BPI), business process redesign, and business reengineering.

G

GIG

"The Global Information Grid is a globally interconnected, end-to-end set of information capabilities enabling the collection, processing, storage, dissemination and management of information. The GIG must be thought of and transformed into a truly global, three-dimensional information processing network by developing and integrating airborne and space-based platform networking and information transport capacity. Integrating systems and networks into a unified global system of systems, makes it easier for authorized users to gain access to information, thus enabling dominant battle space knowledge and decision superiority."

I

ICAM

Integrated Computer-Aided Manufacturing. The ICAM program was helmed in the 1970's by Dennis E. Wisnosky for the United States Air Force. The purpose of the program was to investigate whether manufacturing technologies were delivering the value they promised. The goal was to integrate processes on the factory floor with everything else, from Computer Aided Design (CAD) to inventory and payroll. The ICAM hierarchical "funnel" led to the IDEF "As-Is" / "To-Be" concept that is used in BPR projects today.

IDEF
Integrated DEFinition language.

IDEF Modeling Technique
A combination of graphic and narrative symbols and rules designed to capture the processes and structure of information in an organization. IDEF0 is an activity, or behavior, modeling technique. IDEF1X is a rule, or data, modeling technique.

Wizdom Systems, Inc.'s founder and CEO, Dennis E. Wisnosky, was co-founder of the US Air Force ICAM (Integrated Computer Aided DEFinition) Program and developed the program's IDEF modeling techniques. IDEF models are often the basis for process improvement. Wizdom offers training courses on IDEF Modeling Technique.

IEEE 1471
This document describes a model of activities to produce IT-architecture descriptions in a stakeholder oriented way. The model also covers the use of the IT-architecture descriptions by the stakeholders.

Integrated-Computer Aided Software Engineering (I-CASE)
A set of software design and development tools operating with an integrated shared repository to support the entire systems development life cycle.

Information
1. Knowledge derived from study.

2. Knowledge of a specific event or situation; intelligence.

3. A collection of facts or data: statistical information.

4. The act of informing or the condition of being informed; communication of knowledge: (i.e.: "Safety instructions are provided for the information of our passengers.")

5. Computer Science. A non-accidental signal or character used as an input to a computer or communications system.

6. A numerical measure of the uncertainty of an experimental outcome.

Ishikawa Fishbone
(See Cause and Effect Diagram)

ISO 9000

Family of quality management and quality assurance standards adopted by ISO (International Organization for Standardization, founded 1947), an international consensus of over 110 countries. ISO 9000, first published in 1987, has been adopted as national standards in more than 80 countries.

Job
A job within an organization is made up of four categories of work: mission tasks, initiatives, reactive work, and administrative tasks. Mission tasks are the core and essential purpose of the job. Initiatives are planned efforts to improve job performance or correct a problem in the work environment. Reactive work is not planned by the jobholder and not part of the organization's improvement plan. Administrative tasks comprise the "all other" category of work.

Just in time
A policy calling for the delivery of material, products or services at the time they are needed in an activity or process to reduce inventory, wait time and spoilage.

Key Performance Indicator (KPI)
KPIs are quantitative measures of the performance of a process, activity or function carried out by a business. Standard KPIs are measures of cost, quality and time.

Comparison of AS-IS and TO-BE KPIs for a given process in an Enterprise Architecture tells the architect the potential performance improvement which will be achieved during transformation.

Key Performance Parameter (KPP)
"Those minimum attributes or characteristics considered most essential for an effective military capability. KPPs are validated by the JROC for JROC interest documents, by the Functional Capabilities Board for Joint Impact documents, and by the DoD Component for Joint Integration or Independent documents. CDD and CPD KPPs are included verbatim in the Acquisition Program Baseline. (CJCSI 3170.01C)"

Knowledge
The state or fact of knowing. Familiarity, awareness, or understanding gained through experience or study.

Knowledge Acquisition
The procedure in artificial intelligence of interacting with an external source, usually a domain expert, to find and organize knowledge for the purpose of transferring the knowledge to an expert system to solve problems.

Knowledge Base
From DISA/CIM: A logical collection of information in a particular domain that has been formalized in the appropriate representation with which to perform reasoning. A dynamic knowledge base is used to store

information relevant to solving a particular problem and varies from one problem solving session to the next.

Knowledge-Base of Knowledge
This is the collection of things that are known about a body of study. For instance, the knowledge about trauma care.

Knowledge Base Management System
Pro-active, event driven, rule based.

Knowledge (Explicit)
Specific information about something.

Knowledge (Implicit)
The sum or range of what has been perceived, discovered, or learned.

Knowledge Management
The leveraging of collective wisdom to increase responsiveness and innovation.

Knowledge Store
The collection of the Knowedgebase of the Consolidated Tool Model, Domain Knowledgebase and toolset knowledgebase. This Store contains the data and the "engine" necessary to access that data.

Management Systems

Software tools for supporting the modeling, analysis, and enactment of business processes.

Meta Model
From Oracle publication on CASE: The meta model describes the structure of the Data Model by defining entities, attributes and relationships.

Method
From KFI/HII Methods Team: Regular and systematic means of enterprise improvement including procedures and techniques appropriate to the health care industry.<p>A representation of a complex, real-world phenomenon such that it can answer questions about the real-world phenomenon within some acceptable and predictable tolerance.

NCW
Network Centric Warfare is defined as "an information superiority-enabled concept of operations that generates increased combat power by networking sensors, decision makers, and shooters to achieve shared awareness, increased speed of command, higher tempo of operations, greater lethality, increased survivability, and a degree of self-synchronization."

Net-Ready Key Performance Parameter (NR-KPP)

Replaces the Interoperability KPP "The NR-KPP assesses information needs, information timeliness, information assurance, and net-ready attributes required for both the technical exchange of information and the end-to-end operational effectiveness of that exchange. The NR-KPP consists of verifiable performance measures and associated metrics required to evaluate the timely, accurate, and complete exchange and use of information to satisfy information needs for a given capability (CJCSI 3170.01C)."

Nominal Group Technique (NGT)
A structured brainstorming technique that allows a group or team to quickly come to consensus on the importance of issues, problems or solutions. Based on individual contributions, equal footing of team members and prioritization of issues.

Wizdom's Process Analysis & Redesign training course teaches how to determine priorities for problems and processes with the Nominal Group Technique.

Non Value Added Activity
An activity performed in a process that does not add value to the output product or service, which may or may not have a valid business reason for being performed.

Normalization and (3NF)

Normalization is used in IDEF1X. In relational database management, normalization breaks down data into record groups for efficient processing. There are six stages. By the third stage (third normal form or 3NF), data are identified only by the key field in their record. For example, ordering information is identified by order number, and customer information, by customer number. A major goal of normalization is to eliminate redundancy by having a data element represented in only one place.

OASIS BCM
The purpose of the OASIS Business-Centric Methodology (BCM) TC is to develop a specification which will provide business managers with a set of clearly defined methods with which to acquire agile and interoperable e-business information systems within communities of interests

Object
From DISA/CIM: An object is a package of information and a description of its manipulation...an object comprises a data structure definition and its defined procedures in a single structure....objects are instances of a class, each instance having its own private instance variables...Each object can have various attributes associated with it. Attributes can be local to that object or inherited from the parent object.

Object Modeling
From DISA/CIM: The objective of object modeling is to understand and describe an environment in terms of its objects while embracing the concepts of abstraction, encapsulation, modularity, hierarchy, typing, concurrence and persistence.

Object-Oriented (Development)
From DISA/CIM: An approach to developing software where every component represents an object in the real world, its attributes, and its possible actions; objects can be grouped together into classes to facilitate attribute and action assignments.

OMG-MDA
Model Driven Architecture (MDA) "provides an open, vendor-neutral approach to the challenge of interoperability, building upon and leveraging the value of OMG's established modeling standards: Unified Modeling Language (UML); Meta-Object Facility (MOF); and Common Warehouse Meta-model (CWM). Platform-independent Application descriptions built using these modeling standards can be realized using any major open or proprietary platform, including CORBA, Java, .NET, XMI/XML, and Web-Based platforms."

Organize
To arrange by systematic planning.

Organization
The condition or manner or being organized.

Organization Diagnostics
The process of identifying organization problems with individuals, processes, procedures, technology, culture, etc.

Performance Goals
Performance Goals are standards for the day-to-day operation of the organization's work processes. Well-developed Performance Goals are defined one per each business process, are established based on customer requirements, define performance for each organizational unit and individual jobholder, and provide easily obtained data that clearly shows actual performance against goals.

Performance Measure
An indicator that can be used to evaluate quality, cost, or cycle time characteristics of an activity or process usually against a target or standard value.

Portal
An internet browser combined with a search engine.

Present Value
The current value of a future series of cash flow given a discount factor or interest value. Used to evaluate the alternative investments.

Process
1. A systematic series of actions directed to some end. 2. A continuous action, operation, or series of changes taking place in a definite manner. (e.g., getting to a destination = process performed by a pilot).

Process Model
Also Activity Model - A graphic representation of a business process that exhibits the activities and their interdependencies that make up the business process to any desired level of detail. An activity model reveals the interactions between activities in terms of inputs and outputs while showing the controls placed on each activity and the types of resources assigned to each activity. Wizdom offers a training course in IDEF Activity modeling ProcessWorks! process and activity modeling software.

Process Portal
Software, which focuses the user of the Portal to the explicit knowledge, required to solve his/her particular problem, or dealing with a particular situation or series of events. Changes Implicit Knowledge to Explicit Knowledge.

Quality Function Deployment (QFD)
A requirements identification analysis, flow down, and tracking technique. It focuses on quality and

communication to translate customer needs into product-and-process-design specifics. Also known as the "house of quality." Wizdom's QualWIZard BPR Analysis Tool helps you answer the relationship between your business activities and customer expectations.

Redesign
Business Process Redesign (BPR) The transformation of a business process to achieve significant levels of improvement in one or more performance measures relating to fitness for purpose, quality, cycle times, and cost by using the techniques of streamlining and removing non-value added activities and costs. Redesign projects typically take about six months to complete.

Wizdom offers WizdomWorks! BPR Software, BPR Consulting, and BPR Training Courses.

Reengineering
Business Process Reengineering (BPR) and Redesign.

RM-ODP
Reference Model for Open Distributed Systems - a co-coordinating framework for the standardization of Open Distributed Processing (ODP).

Repository

A mechanism for storing any information that has to do with the definition of a system at any point in its life cycle. Repository services would typically be provided for extensibility, recovery, integrity, naming standards and a wide variety of other management functions.

Resource
An object in competition with another like object. A scarce object.

S.A.I.L.
A public/private partnership that helps establish normalized architecture nomenclature (terms and diagrams) to better enable the communication of business need to technical solutions. A solution architecture market exchange where buyers and suppliers can better serve the Value Chain in an open and conflict free environment.

Stove Pipe
Term commonly used to reflect that a business function operates in a vertically integrated manner, but does not interact efficiently or effectively with related functions. (e.g., Human Resources does not work with training).

Strategic Business Process Reengineering (SBPR)
(See Business Architecture Modernization (BAM))

TO-BE Model
Models that are the result of applying improvement opportunities to the current (AS-IS) business environment.

> (See WizdomWorks! BPR Software, Wizdom BPR Training Courses, and Wizdom Consulting Services.)

TOGAF
TOGAF, The Open Group Architecture Framework, is an industry standard architecture framework that may be used freely by any organization wishing to develop an information systems architecture for use within that organization.

Topic Area
A cross-functional grouping of business areas (grouping of processes). Topic areas include but are not limited to Admissions and Classification, Communication, Custody, Employment and Education, Services, Substance Abuse.

Total Quality Management/Total Quality Leadership (TQM/TQL)
Both a philosophy and a set of guiding principles that represent the foundation of the continuously improving organization. TQM/TQL is the application of quantitative methods and human resources to improve the material and services supplied to a organization, all the processes within

an organization, and the degree to which the needs of the customer are met, now and in the future. TQM/TQL integrates fundamental management techniques, existing improvement efforts and technical tools under a disciplined approach focused on continuous improvement.
(See Wizdom's QualWIZard analysis tool for simple quality solutions.)

Trigger
The precedence with respect to time between activity types.

Use Case Diagram (UCD)
One of five types of behavior diagrams specified within the Universal Modeling Language (UML). A UCD shows a systems function from a users point of view. Ivar Jacobson is credited with the Use Case concept.

Value Added Activity
An activity in a process that adds value to an output product or service, that is, the activity merits the cost of the resources it consumes in production.

Variable Cost

A cost element that varies directly with the amount of product or service produced by an activity or cost. Variable costs go to zero if the activity stops.

Workflow
A system whose elements are activities, related to one another by a trigger relation, and triggered by external events, which represent a business process starting with a commitment and ending with the termination of that commitment.

Workflow Management Systems
Integrated software tools for supporting the modeling, analysis, and enactment of business processes.
Wizdom's FlowWIZard analysis tool helps you perform real-world work flow analysis.

Index

3NF, 249, 250
5.11.1 Physical Schema, viii, 77, 149, 155, 156, 167, 187, 188, 189
Activity, vii, viii, ix, 51, 52, 58, 64, 66, 75, 76, 77, 80, 94, 95, 96, 97, 99, 100, 102, 117, 118, 119, 120, 121, 139, 176, 178, 200, 214, 229, 253
Activity Based Costing, 96, 229
Activity Model, vii, viii, 51, 58, 66, 75, 80, 94, 95, 102, 117, 118, 119, 120, 176, 178, 229, 253
Actor, 230
Annual Operating Plan, 230
Application Program Interface, 230
Architecture, 230
AS-IS Model, 230
Attribute, 231
Baseline, 231
Benchmarking, 231
Best Practice, 232
Born Joint, 31, 33, 34, 42, 43, 86, 165, 169
BPR - definition, 233, 241
Business Architecture Modernization, 232, 255
Business Case, 232
Business Management Modernization Program, 207
Business Objectives, 233
Business Process Improvement, 233
Business Process Management Initiative, 231
Business Process Portal, 233
Business Process Redesign – a definition, 233, 254
Business Process Reengineering, xi, xv,

xvi, 19, 20, 21, 36, 44, 46, 90, 94, 95, 208, 229, 230, 232, 233, 234, 236, 240, 243, 254, 255, 256

Business Process Reengineering - definition, 233, 241

CADM, vii, 53, 102, 103, 104, 128, 234

Cause and Effect Diagram, 235, 244

Clinger-Cohen Act, 19, 20, 21, 26, 30, 85, 94, 101, 118

Command, Control, Communications, Computers, Intelligence, Surveillance, and Reconnaissance (C4ISR) Architecture Framework, 19, 29, 31, 44, 73, 87, 110, 234

Component Based Architecture, 27

Consolidated Tool Model, 235, 247

Continuous Process Improvement, 235

CostWizard, 222, 229

Cross Functional Process Improvement, 236

Customer, v, 31, 32, 35, 37, 39, 40, 43, 59, 78, 96, 97, 158, 170, 231, 236, 250, 252, 254, 257

Data – a definition, 236

Data Model – a definition, 237

Data Passive, 237

Data Repository, 237

Database, 236

Database Management Systems Object, 237

DataWorks!, 167, 226, 228

Defense Information Systems Agency, 238, 239, 246, 250, 251

Dennis E. Wisnosky, 1, xi, xiv, 72, 208, 209, 242, 243

Discounted Cash Flow, 238

Doctrine, Organization, Training, Materiel, Leadership and education, Personnel and Facilities, 37, 38
DoD Architecture Framework, 18, 30, 31
DoDAF products, xvi, 32, 38, 40, 44, 46, 51, 52, 59, 85, 103, 118, 172
Domain, 236, 238
Economic Analysis, 239
Enterprise, 239
Enterprise Architecture, 1, vi, xvii, 18, 19, 22, 23, 24, 29, 35, 49, 51, 59, 72, 75, 87, 106, 158, 160, 163, 207, 218
Entity, 240
Event, 240
Explicit Knowledge, 247
Extensibility, 240
Federal Enterprise Architecture, 18, 19, 22, 26, 27, 28, 29, 31, 43, 232, 241
Field, 240
Fixed Cost, 241
Function, 241
Functional Capabilities Board, 36, 41, 42, 246
Functional Economic Analysis, 232, 241
Functional Process Improvement, 233, 234, 241
Global Information Grid, 19, 212, 242
High-Level Operational Concept Graphic, vii, ix, 51, 57, 74, 109, 110, 111, 121, 167, 172, 173, 174, 183, 189
IDEF Modeling Technique, 243
implementing part or all of a database, 240
Implicit Knowledge, 247
Information – a definition, 244
Integrated Computer Aided Manufacturing

Program, xi, xiv, xv, 22, 53, 242, 243
Integrated Computer-Aided Manufacturing, xi, xiv, xv, 22, 53, 242, 243
Integrated Definition Language, v, vi, xiv, 46, 53, 56, 60, 61, 65, 74, 103, 108, 172, 211, 229, 243, 253
Integrated Dictionary, vii, viii, 51, 56, 64, 68, 107, 108, 109, 120, 128, 167, 170, 171, 172, 178, 183
Integrated-Computer Aided Software Engineering, 244
Ishikawa Fishbone, 235, 244
ISO 9000, 244, 245
JCIDS Gatekeeper, 41
Job – a definition, 245
Joint Capabilities Integration and Development System, xvii
Joint Technical Architecture, 158, 204
Joseph Vogel, 1
Just in time, 245
Key Interface Profiles, 87, 88, 90
Key Performance Indicator, v, vii, 85, 90, 94, 95, 96, 97, 100, 101, 102, 177, 181, 245
Key Performance Parameter, vi, vii, 58, 85, 87, 88, 89, 90, 177, 212, 246, 249
Knowledge – a definition, 246
Knowledge Acquisition, 246
Knowledge Base Management System, 247
Knowledge Base, a definition, 246
Knowledge Management – a definition, 247
Knowledge Store, 247

Knowledge-Base of Knowledge, 247
Logical Data Model, viii, ix, 60, 61, 70, 77, 122, 127, 128, 129, 156, 167, 185, 187, 188, 189, 223
Management Systems, 248, 258
Mandroid, 175, 215
Marshall Field, 32
Meta Model – a definition, 248
Method, 248
Minimalist Methodology, v, vi, viii, xiv, xvii, 43, 44, 46, 51, 52, 55, 57, 58, 73, 78, 101, 103, 106, 162, 165, 166, 168, 169, 183, 204
Model Driven Architecture, 251
Net-Ready Key Performance Parameter (NR-KPP), 212, 248
Network Centric Warfare, 19, 208, 248
Nominal Group Technique, 249
Non Value Added Activity, 249
Normalization, 249, 250
OASIS Business-Centric Methodology, 18, 250
Object – a definition, 250
Object Modeling – a definition, 251
Object-Oriented Development, 251
Operational Activity Model, vii, viii, ix, 51, 56, 60, 61, 66, 74, 75, 80, 94, 95, 101, 102, 105, 112, 116, 117, 118, 119, 120, 121, 123, 128, 129, 136, 138, 150, 167, 176, 177, 178, 179, 180, 181, 183, 185, 186, 189, 192, 196, 197, 198, 199, 200
Operational Activity to Systems Function Traceability Matrix, viii, 52, 136, 137,

138, 139, 167, 200, 201, 202
Operational Event-Trace Description, ix, 52, 116, 125, 138, 167, 189, 190, 193
Operational Information Exchange Matrix, vii, ix, 51, 85, 86, 113, 114, 128, 140, 167, 191, 193
Operational Node Connectivity Description, vii, 51, 81, 86, 87, 110, 111, 112, 113, 116, 121, 130, 132, 167, 196, 197
Operational Rules Model, viii, ix, 60, 66, 116, 121, 122, 123, 149, 167, 192
Operational State Transition Description, viii, ix, 78, 101, 116, 123, 124, 125, 138, 167, 193, 194, 195
Organization – a definition, 252
Organization Diagnostics, 252
Organizational Relationships Chart, viii, ix, 52, 74, 77, 115, 116, 121, 167, 184, 188, 189, 196
Organize – a definition, 251
Overview and Summary Information, vii, viii, 51, 56, 62, 103, 104, 105, 106, 107, 167, 169, 170, 172, 174, 176
Performance Goals, 252
Performance Measure, 252
Portal – a definition, 252
Present Value, 252
Process – a definition, 253
Process Model – a definition, 229, 253
Process Models to Data Models, 219
Process Portal – a definition, 253

ProcessWorks!, 119, 167, 176, 229, 253
Quality Function Deployment, 253
QualWIZard, 254, 257
Ralph Waldo Emerson, 44, 71
Reengineering, 254
Reference Model for Open Distributed Systems, 18, 254
Repository – a definition, 255
Resource – a definition, 255
Rumsfeld, 207
S.A.I.L. -, 18, 255
Sir Winston Churchill, 18, 206
Stove Pipe, 34, 236, 255
Strategic Business Process Reengineering, 255
Symbology, vi, vii, 71, 74, 76, 77, 79, 80, 81, 82, 83, 84
Systems Communications Description, viii, 52, 131, 132, 133, 134, 138, 142, 149, 150
Systems Data Exchange Matrix, viii, ix, 52, 85, 86, 139, 140, 141, 142, 167, 201, 202
Systems Event-Trace Description, viii, ix, 148, 153, 154, 155, 167, 190, 193, 195
Systems Evolution Description, viii, 143, 144, 145, 146, 147, 160
Systems Interface Description, viii, ix, 51, 77, 78, 82, 121, 129, 130, 131, 132, 133, 134, 138, 142, 148, 149, 150, 152, 153, 154, 155, 156, 167, 187, 188, 189, 190, 193, 194, 195, 198, 199, 202, 203
Systems Performance Parameters Matrix, viii, 141, 142, 143, 144
Systems Rules Model, viii, 148, 149, 150

Systems State Transition Description, viii, 78, 148, 150, 152, 153, 154, 167, 194, 195
Systems Technology Forecast, viii, 143, 144, 146, 147, 148, 160
Systems-Systems Matrix, viii, 52, 133, 134, 135
Technical Standards Forecast, viii, 144, 147, 160, 161
The Open Group Architecture Framework, 18, 256
TO-BE Model – a definition, 256
Topic Area, 256
Total Quality Management/Total Quality Leadership, 256
Trigger, 79, 257, 258
UCD, 74, 257
UML, v, vi, vii, viii, xvi, 44, 46, 52, 53, 54, 56, 58, 71, 72, 73, 75, 76, 77, 78, 79, 80, 81, 82, 83, 84, 103, 108, 113, 117, 118, 120, 129, 131, 133, 134, 162, 179, 181, 182, 211, 251, 257
Use Case Diagram, vi, 74, 75, 119, 257
Value Added Activity, 257
Value Added Activity – a definition, 257
Variable Cost, 257
W. Edwards Deming, 210
Wizdom Systems, Inc., 2, xi, xii, xvii, 209, 214, 243
WizdomWorks!, ix, 218, 221, 222, 228, 230, 234, 254, 256
Woodrow Wilson, 32
Workflow, 20, 216, 217, 218, 258
Workflow Management Systems, 258
Yogi Berra, 85